THE REVOLUTION OF 1688

Whig Triumph or Palace Revolution?

PROBLEMS IN EUROPEAN CIVILIZATION

UNDER THE EDITORIAL DIRECTION OF

Ralph W. Greenlaw* and Dwight E. Lee†

Other volumes in preparation

PROBLEMS IN EUROPEAN CIVILIZATION

THE
REVOLUTION OF 1688

Whig Triumph or Palace Revolution?

EDITED WITH AN INTRODUCTION BY

Gerald M. Straka

MICHIGAN STATE UNIVERSITY   OAKLAND

D. C. HEATH AND COMPANY · BOSTON

Table of Contents

v

PART III: RECENT ANTI–WHIG REVISIONS AND RESTORATIONS

Introduction

THE Revolution of 1688 is the culmination of the seventeenth-century struggle between parliament and the Stuarts over the issue of sovereignty. From the time James I came to the throne in 1603, legislature and crown debated and fought over which of them had ultimate control over the making of law. At times, as under Charles I and Strafford, the crown claimed and exercised the right; under Cromwell, parliament triumphed. When the later Stuarts, Charles II and James II, attempted to match and then outdo their father in destroying parliamentary sovereignty, the Whigs and a majority of the Tories withdrew their support. Seven leading lords made plans to exclude the Stuart family altogether. It is their invitation to James II's nephew, William of Orange, his acceptance of the proffered crown, and the laws made by William and parliament after 1688 that constituted the basic theme of the "bloodless revolution."

The Revolution, then as now, impresses students of history with its simplicity. It exhibits none of the complexities of the rebellion of 1643 or of the French Revolution a century later, for it consists mainly of one movement: the peaceful accession of the House of Orange. It is not a mass movement, nor a class movement; individuals from many parties contributed to its success. It is not a "revolution" as that word is used today, for it resulted in a body of laws which strengthened rather than overthrew the old order. If any innovations can be found, they consist in the granting of toleration to dissenters, the regularization of parliamentary elections,

and the establishment of a Protestant monarchy. The Revolution, then, means nothing more than that the English rejected a specific man as unfit to rule, repudiated his foreign and domestic policy, and got themselves a king who pleased them better.

Then why do historians give a significant place to a "palace revolution"? Precisely because parliament was able to make such a choice. When the Convention Parliament met in February, 1689, it declared that James II had "abdicated" when he escaped to France, but regardless of the explanation parliament assumed that it had the power to replace one king by another. Here was an ultimate power over the throne — the power of deposition. Furthermore, many have assumed, then and now, that parliament's grant of the throne to William implied that the use of kingly prerogatives in the future would be a trust given by parliament; since parliament represented the people of England, ultimate governmental power was believed to be the people's. Thus the Revolution of 1688 has come to mean, through implication, that modern political democracy and limited monarchy begin with the Revolution Settlement.

Still, it must be remembered that these last-mentioned interpretations have meaning only through implication. This was not a democratic revolution, for it safeguarded rights only to those who had them before 1688 — the nobles and landowners of England. There is little to distinguish this event from the battle the barons waged with King John; in spirit the Bill of Rights resembles Magna Carta more than it does the Declaration of Independence. One thing only distinguishes the Glorious Revolution from earlier constitutional conflicts between the king and his leading subjects: this was to be the last struggle over the mediaeval problem of sovereignty in England. Politically speaking, the Middle Ages in England do not end in 1485 but in 1688; only after this date do the English begin to occupy themselves with perfecting the cabinet system, parliamentary reform, and extending the franchise, having finally declared that the king is not the sole source of law.

Historical interpretations of the Revolution appeared immediately in the wake of the events of 1688. The first part of this collection, "Contemporary Combatants and Commentators," begins with eyewitness accounts and views which mingle fact and propaganda. Each essay was selected to present a differing view, the whole representing the milieu of reaction to William III's reign. The variety of reactions can be explained by the fact that little was done to prepare men for the Revolution, and with its sudden termination in the crowning of William and Mary, the fight for the Revolution began, not in the field, but in pamphlets and books. The Revolution of 1688 is consequently a rare event in that its rationalization postdates its occurrence.

John Evelyn's account of the Revolution opens the first part. At this point in Evelyn's life — he was sixty-eight — the world had been turned upside down too many times for him to be awed by a bloodless *coup*. Evelyn retains his composure throughout, though surprised at many sudden turns of events. His faith in the *via media* of Anglicanism, the same faith of the revolutionaries, leaves him with little doubt that the solution will be a sane one. Evelyn knew the participants too well to be overly worried, and though he had the Anglican's dread of rebellion and disobedience to his king, he could not but be glad to be rid of a popish prince.

With the selection by Gilbert Burnet,

propagandist for Prince William, we see a revolutionary manifesto. It was published on the eve of the calling of the Convention Parliament and was addressed to moderate, rational minds. Compared with the manifestoes of later revolutions, this is a dull one. There is no emotionalism, no appeal to "man the barricades," which attests to the character of what one author calls the "respectable revolution." Nonetheless, it is a far more relevant document than the famous work by Locke, for as the reader will learn, Locke wrote his *Treatise on Government* before the Revolution, never intending to justify the Revolution after it happened, while Burnet's justification was written just as William of Orange entered London. Like Locke, Burnet believes in the inviolability of property, for by property man makes his living in the world. No king has a right to deprive subjects of their property, since it would be tantamount to depriving them of life; and life, like liberty, is a natural right. Kings retain their authority only as they effectively safeguard property and liberty. Burnet concludes by asking Englishmen whether James has done either.

The next pamphlet represents the position of those who regarded the Revolution as a monstrous piece of treachery. The Jacobites (for *Jacobus,* Latin for James) appeared as a political movement during the debates in the parliament that William of Orange called. When parliament voted to confer the crown on William and Mary, they still pursued their purpose of restoring James, forming an underground movement which was to last for more than fifty years. This anonymous Jacobite pamphlet denounces the Revolution on a number of important counts: the parliament which William called is illegal and its acts without sanction, for it was not summoned by the king; the removal of James from the throne is illegal and immoral; the Revolution furthers the aspirations of the hated republicans. The author is fair enough to admit that James acted beyond the limit of the law, though excusing him because he was king. But what excuse, he asks, can parliament claim for its illegal actions? Interestingly enough, he agrees with those who interpreted the Revolution as a break in the social contract between king and people, but whereas the Whig contractarians believed James had caused it by "deserting" his kingdom, the Jacobites insisted that the Convention Parliament broke the contract by convening without warrant from the rightful king.

For the left wing, we have two republican tracts. Unlike the works that appeared in Cromwell's time, however, these are far less militant. The writers ask for little more than a limited monarchy and a better-defined constitution. Students of the nineteenth century will recognize some demands that Chartists will make: salaries for members of parliament, annual elections and meetings, broadening of the franchise. A few proposals go beyond these, such as the demand for removal of the royal veto and the right of parliament to call and dissolve itself. The most interesting suggestion is that the Convention be turned into a constituent assembly with powers to write a new constitution for the realm, a single document of state. But such an action was not to be taken until a century later after another revolution by Englishmen in America. The English constitution was to remain the bewildering mass of precedent, law, and opinion it is to this day.

Bishop William Lloyd presents a view of the Revolution which, unfortunately, is rarely given either credence or recognition by modern historians. His was an interpretation common at the time, especially among conservative supporters of the Revolution. Briefly, Lloyd thought that God had brought about the Revolution and that William's government should therefore be regarded as having divine right. Before 1688 the Anglican church preached the divinity of hereditary right, and when parliament ignored it, the conservatives adjusted their views by declaring that William's right by conquest was

as good as a hereditary title. Anglicans also modified the precept that the king is accountable only to God for his rule. Clearly, James, an evil king who had misused his trust, had been judged unfit by God, who raised William of Orange, His avenger, to save English Protestantism and liberty. These views will hardly satisfy the modern reader, but recalling the essential piety of the age and the necessity for believing in divine right in some form, this rationality will be seen to have its place. If the Anglican was forced to believe that the Revolution destroyed divine right theory, he would have to admit that when James II left England, he took godly rule with him.

When John Locke published his *Treatise* in 1690, it came out as one of scores of such works, justifying revolution on the basis of natural right and the civil contract. Time and posterity have proved it the best statement of natural liberty. That it was written before 1688 is irrelevant, considering that succeeding generations have cherished Locke as the great champion who justified the Revolution for the Whig party and its middle-class adherents. His was to be the best-remembered interpretation of the civil contract; and even though he conceived it in Charles II's reign, its theme was amply suited to the deposition of any paternalistic prince.

Part II, "The Triumph of Whig Theory in Modern Interpretation," indicates how three Whig historians have tried to relate the Glorious Revolution to liberal and democratic developments in the modern world. They see 1688 as the beginning of parliamentary supremacy and the rule of law; above all, they see it as the final repudiation of tyranny in England. Although they agree that it was not a real revolution, the Revolution ultimately resulted in revolutionary changes, for they maintain that modern parliamentary democracy could not have arrived without some dramatic incident demonstrating the power of parliament over the crown. The Glorious Revolution placed government in the hands of parliament; the future would place parliament in the hands of the people.

To Thomas Babington Macaulay, writing in the mid-nineteenth century, the history of modern Britain began with the Revolution, for from that date free trade linked with free thought expressed in a free parliament had grown to make England the envy of the world. So obvious was this theme that Macaulay's history becomes merely the telling of a story, the whole work a philosophy of liberalism. The charm his narrative retains is in his unqualified acceptance of the goodness of the present and the perfection he expected in the future.

George Macaulay Trevelyan continues the eulogistic tradition in Revolution historiography. Again we have history told as manifest destiny, but this time for the twentieth-century reader. Just as Macaulay showed how England was the first to achieve free representative government one hundred years ahead of the rest of the world, Trevelyan handles the theme of democratic unification and its first appearance in England. The Revolution becomes the great bonding agent, for before 1688 the land was divided, interest against interest, class against class; after the Revolution, one consciousness emerged, and its voice was that of parliament. Civil war was superseded by debate, and debate is the democratic methodology produced by the "bloodless revolution." Trevelyan is the writer most responsible for the belief that the Bill of Rights forced the monarch to accept the civil contract as a binding pledge upon the king to rule with responsibility to his people, whereas in point of fact the contract never became part of the English constitution, being omitted before the Bill of Rights became law. Nevertheless, Trevelyan succeeds as no one before him in relating the Revolution to the development of modern democracy.

David Ogg's work in late seventeenth-century history is among the most thoughtful. He has analyzed the Revolution from the point of view of its precedents and its antecedents, its causes and effects, successfully relating it to the whole scope of English history. His sense of institutional continuity makes the reader aware that the Revolution concentrated in itself all the major features of English public life, resolving mediaeval contradictions, at the same time creating new opportunities and problems for the future.

In the past number of years, a few historians have been at work revising Whig viewpoints, in many cases restoring lost causes and lost viewpoints for the modern reader's consideration. Thus the third section is called "Recent Anti-Whig Revisions and Restorations." One author restores the Jacobites to their rightful place as an effective third force between Tories and Whigs; another removes the notion, long cherished, that John Locke deliberately set out to justify the Revolution for the Whigs after it took place; another writer goes so far as to conclude that the Revolution was not, as the Whigs maintain, a true revolution which resulted in a liberal establishment, but a successfully engineered capture of the throne by a strong-willed and rather illiberal conqueror. Finally, the last essay tries to revise the Whig notion that the hated divine right of kings theory died in 1688 by pointing out that divine right was used to justify the events of that year and that the new regime could not have done without it.

George L. Cherry's article on the Jacobites was one of the first revisions of what Herbert Butterfield called "the Whig interpretation of history." It had been customary to treat the Jacobite position with the scorn due any lost cause, but Cherry raises the possibility that the Jacobite position is worthy of a real place in Revolution theory. Not only were their arguments sounder than those of most of their critics during the discussions in the Convention Parliament, but their position might well have become the majority view if the Whigs and Tories had not hurried the debate to a sudden conclusion. Cherry's willingness to give the Jacobites a hearing is more than refreshing; it is sound scholarship.

Peter Laslett's task has been to sever the historical connection between John Locke and the Glorious Revolution. Locke has always been the philosopher of revolutionary theory. Laslett announces, however, that Locke had not intended to justify the Revolution *ex post facto,* and that he probably wrote the *Two Treatises of Government* to justify Whig policy, not as it related to the Revolution, but to the exclusion controversy (the attempt at the end of Charles II's reign to exclude James from the succession), which ended eight years earlier. When the work finally was published in 1690, its principles were incorrectly taken to apply to the Revolution. The detective work Laslett employs to uncover this connection is among the finest in scholarly reconstruction.

The selection from Mrs. Pinkham's book represents the most radical reappraisal of the Revolution. William of Orange and not parliament occupies the center of the stage as the author indicates how William planned, directed, and fulfilled his lifelong wish to become king of England. Heretofore the Prince of Orange was seen as a passive participant in what parliament did, being interested only in gaining the throne in order to bring England into his continental alliance against Louis XIV. After Mrs. Pinkham's analysis, the Revolution is placed in a new perspective and becomes little more than an old-fashioned act of conquest by a usurping prince.

The final selection, written by the editor, presents what he feels was the most common contemporaneous interpretation of the Revolution. It has often been said that when William accepted a parliamentary title to the throne, no one could believe any longer in the divine right of kingship. His contention is that the Revolution and William III had to be accepted on divine-right terms, for the older generation could not dissociate divinity from the

monarchical system. The pious Anglicans made modifications in their thinking about divine right, but they continued to believe that William's crown was as sacred as James's had been. If one looks at the Revolution through their eyes, it is more like the triumph of a Biblical king than the emergence of a mercantilist monarch and a class interested in protecting its property.

The nineteenth-century commentator Walter Bagehot spoke of 1688 as "the minimum of a revolution, because in law, at least, it only changed the dynasty, but exactly on that account it was the greatest shock to the common multitude, who see the dynasty but see nothing else." [1] A major problem that grows out of this statement is Bagehot's interpretation of the Revolution as only a change in dynasty. If this is all that occurred, one can safely say that it was a palace revolution. But, as indicated at the beginning of this introduction, many writers have seen much more in this event. The term "Revolution Settlement" is frequently used to describe all the acts passed by parliament after William became king. Thus if the Revolution is to assume a greater meaning than dynastic change, we must include not only the "deposition" of James II but the settlement that grew out of it: the Bill of Rights, the Toleration Act, the Triennial Act, and all the acts up to and including the Act of Settlement of 1701. Much of the conflict of opinion that arises over the Revolution is based on these two interpretations of the events of 1688, so that if a writer confines his view to the nine months it took William to become king and focuses only on his actions, the affair is a dynastic change. If another sees the Revolution as the central point of a much larger manifestation, the end of absolutism and the rise of democracy and the limited monarch, he will see 1688 as a Whig triumph and a major step toward the future liberal state. The truth may lie somewhere between.

[1] In his *The English Constitution* (London, 1955), p. 251.

A CHRONOLOGY OF THE REVOLUTION ERA

N.B. England did not adopt the Gregorian or New Style calendar until 1752, whereas most continental countries had used it since 1582. The English use of the Julian or Old Style calendar frequently necessitated a double reckoning, since, in the seventeenth century, the Julian calendar was ten days behind the Gregorian. Furthermore, the new year was usually regarded in England as starting on March 25. Thus dates were frequently given: $\frac{5}{15}$ January 168$\frac{8}{9}$. The following table is in the New Style.

1679	3 February: Charles II's Long Parliament dissolved after eighteen years. Exclusion controversy begins over the exclusion of James, Duke of York, from the succession.
1679–1681	Three parliaments are held and dissolved over the exclusion issue. Habeas Corpus Act passed in 1679 by parliament.
1681	7 April: Charles II dissolves the Oxford parliament, having been freed of financial dependence by a grant from Louis XIV. Shaftesbury and Whigs flee to Holland. Locke completes work on *Two Treatises of Government* in Holland.
1685	16 February: Charles II dies and James II, his brother, succeeds to the throne. James's only parliament summoned and held until July, 1687. Duke of Monmouth attempts to overthrow James.
1686	25 July: a body of Ecclesiastical Commissioners is erected to keep the Church of England under control.
1687	14 April: James's Declaration of Indulgence grants toleration to Catholics and dissenters through decree, making use of the suspending power to suspend the Test Act.
1688	7 May: a second Declaration of Indulgence issued and ordered to be read from every Anglican pulpit. Seven bishops refuse to read it and are arrested for seditious libel; they are found not guilty.
	20 June: a son is born to the queen.
	10 July: Admiral Russell takes an invitation to invade England, signed by seven nobles, to William of Orange.
	11-15 November: William sails from Holland, lands in southwestern England.
1689	2 January: James flees England, after a prior abortive flight, to end his days in France.
	1 February: Convention Parliament meets, draws up Bill of Rights.
	23 February: William and Mary accept the throne. Parliament passes Mutiny Act, Toleration Act.
	17 May: William declares war against Louis XIV.
1690	11 July: Battle of the Boyne River in Ireland marks defeat of James II's attempt to return, safeguards the Revolution.

The Conflict of Opinion

. . . That when such a single person or prince sets up his own arbitrary will in place of the laws which are the will of the society, declared by the legislative, then the legislative is changed. . . . Whoever introduces new laws, not being thereunto authorised by the fundamental appointment of the society, or subverts the old, disowns and overturns the power by which they were made. . . . In these and the like cases, when the government is dissolved, the people are at liberty to provide for themselves by erecting a new legislative, differing from the other, by the change of persons, or form, or both, as they shall find it most for their safety and good.

—John Locke

Here we are, and here we must be eternally, till we learn the wit of a carter, and set the overturned cart on the wheels again; in plain terms, till we re-settle King James on his throne. The happiness of England depends upon a rightful king, we see it always went out with him, and 'tis in vain to hope it ever will, or can return without him. . . . It is demonstration that we cannot recover our old constitution, without our king. It stands upon right of blood, it fell with that right. . . .

—The Jacobite Position

William and Mary were not made King and Queen without conditions. The instrument by which the Convention raised them to the throne was the famous Declaration of Right. It made a long recital of the various illegal acts of James, more especially his claim to suspend the laws by Prerogative; it declared all these actions to have been illegal, and it required the acceptance of these limitations of the royal power by the new sovereigns as a condition of their elevation to the throne.

—George Macaulay Trevelyan

Certainly at no time was the offer of the crown made directly or explicitly contingent upon acceptance of the declaration by William and Mary, and it is hard to find much indication of any implicit or indirect condition. In fact, the Declaration of Rights did not receive its final form nor was it adopted by Parliament and given the validity of royal approval until much later in the year, after William and Mary had been safely crowned for some months. . . . The Declaration of Rights which William and Mary ultimately approved contained no limitations not already in existence. Nor was William accepting any theoretical principle that Parliament had an unlimited right of limitation. He agreed to rule according to the laws of England as every king had done who had ever worn the crown.

—Lucile Pinkham

xiii

The ultimate view that we take of the Revolution of 1688 must be determined by our preference either for royal absolutism or for parliamentary government. James II forced England to choose once for all between these two: he refused to inhabit any half-way house. It was well that the choice had to be made so decisively and so soon. . . .

—GEORGE M. TREVELYAN

. . . most of the old rights [of the king] remained [after the Revolution settlement], including those of summoning, proroguing, and dissolving parliament; dismissing judges (before the Act of Settlement); appointing to high offices of state; vetoing legislation; declaring war and making peace. These were substantial rights. It is one of the paradoxes of English history that the parliamentary constitution dates from an Act which diminished the royal power so little, and from the rule of a king whose prerogatives were so great.

—DAVID OGG

PART I: CONTEMPORARY COMBATANTS AND COMMENTATORS

The Confusion of Events, May, 1688–February, 1689

JOHN EVELYN

While many of Evelyn's works were concerned chiefly with gardening, he is particularly remembered today for his diary, kept from 1640 to his death in 1706. It is an extremely valuable document because Evelyn's place in society allowed him intimacy with many of the great figures of the century. His pacific nature would not allow him to defend Charles I during the civil wars, but in his loyalties he remained a staunch monarchist and served in a number of minor posts under Charles II. His is the outlook of the moderate Tory element which supported the Revolution with lukewarm enthusiasm.

[May 1688] 18th. The King enjoining the ministers to read his Declaration for giving liberty of conscience (as it was styled) in all the churches of England, this evening, six Bishops, Bath and Wells, Peterborough, Ely, Chichester, St. Asaph, and Bristol, in the name of all the rest of the Bishops, came to his Majesty to petition him, that he would not impose the reading of it to the several congregations within their dioceses; not that they were averse to the publishing it for want of due tenderness towards Dissenters, in relation to whom they should be willing to come to such a temper as should be thought fit, when that matter might be considered and settled in Parliament and Convocation; but that, the Declaration being founded on such a dispensing power as might at pleasure set aside all laws ecclesiastical and civil, it appeared to them illegal, as it had done to the Parliament in 1661 and 1672, and that it was a point of such consequence, that they could not so far make themselves par-

ties to it, as the reading of it in church in time of Divine Service amounted to.

The King was so far incensed at this address, that he with threatening expressions commanded them to obey him in reading it at their perils, and so dismissed them. . . .

25th. All the discourse now was about the Bishops refusing to read the injunction for the abolition of the Test, &c. It seems the injunction came so crudely from the Secretary's office, that it was neither sealed nor signed in form, nor had any lawyer been consulted, so as the Bishops, who took all imaginable advice, put the Court to great difficulties how to proceed against them. Great were the consults, and a proclamation was expected all this day; but nothing was done. The action of the Bishops was universally applauded, and reconciled many adverse parties, Papists only excepted, who were now exceedingly perplexed, and violent courses were every moment expected. Report was, that the

From *The Diary of John Evelyn*, edited by William Bray. Everyman's Library. Reprinted by permission of E. P. Dutton and Co., Inc. Vol. II, pp. 276–295.

Protestant secular Lords and Nobility would abet the Clergy. . . .

8th June. This day, the Archbishop of Canterbury, with the Bishops of Ely, Chichester, St. Asaph, Bristol, Peterborough, and Bath and Wells, were sent from the Privy Council prisoners to the Tower, for refusing to give bail for their appearance, on their not reading the Declaration for liberty of conscience; they refused to give bail, as it would have prejudiced their peerage. The concern of the people for them was wonderful, infinite crowds on their knees begging their blessing, and praying for them, as they passed out of the barge along the Tower-wharf.

10th. A *young Prince* born, which will cause disputes.

About two o'clock, we heard the Tower-ordnance discharged, and the bells ring for the birth of a Prince of Wales. This was very surprising, it having been universally given out that her Majesty did not look till the next month. . . .

15th. Being the first day of Term, the Bishops were brought to Westminster on Habeas Corpus, when the indictment was read, and they were called on to plead; their Counsel objected that the warrant was illegal; but, after long debate, it was over-ruled, and they pleaded. The Court then offered to take bail for their appearance; but this they refused, and at last were dismissed on their own recognizances to appear that day fortnight; the Archbishop in £200, the Bishops £100 each. . . .

29th. They appeared; the trial lasted from nine in the morning to past six in the evening, when the Jury retired to consider of their verdict, and the Court adjourned to nine the next morning. The Jury were locked up till that time, eleven of them being for an acquittal; but one (Arnold, a brewer) would not consent. At length he agreed with the others. The Chief Justice, Wright, behaved with great moderation and civility to the Bishops. Alibone, a Papist, was strongly against them; but Holloway and Powell being of opinion in their favour, they were acquitted. When this was heard, there was great rejoicing; and there was a lane of people from the King's Bench to the waterside, on their knees, as the Bishops passed and repassed, to beg their blessing. Bonfires were made that night, and bells rung, which was taken very ill at Court, and an appearance of nearly sixty Earls and Lords, &c., were all along full of comfort and cheerful.

Note, they denied to pay the Lieutenant of the Tower (Hales, who used them very surlily) any fees, alleging that none were due.

The night was solemnized with bonfires, and other fireworks, &c. . . .

12th July. The camp now began at Hounslow;[1] but the nation was in high discontent.

Colonel Titus, Sir Henry Vane (son of him who was executed for his treason), and some other of the Presbyterians and Independent party, were sworn of the Privy Council, from hopes of thereby diverting that party from going over to the Bishops and Church of England, which now they began to do, foreseeing the design of the Papists to descend and take in their most hateful of heretics (as they at other times expressed them to be) to effect their own ends, now evident; the utter extirpation of the Church of England first, and then the rest would follow. . . .

10th August. Dr. Tenison now told me there would suddenly be some great thing discovered. This was the Prince of Orange intending to come over. . . .

23rd August. . . . Dr. Sprat, Bishop of Rochester, wrote a very honest and handsome letter to the Commissioners Ecclesiastical, excusing himself from sitting any longer among them, he by no means approving of their prosecuting the Clergy who refused to read the Declaration for liberty of conscience, in prejudice of the Church of England.

The Dutch make extraordinary prepara-

[1] The army encampment set up by James outside of London, officered by Catholics, to discourage popular demonstrations against his policies. [Editor's note]

tions both at sea and land, which with the no small progress Popery makes among us, puts us to many difficulties. The Popish Irish soldiers commit many murders and insults; the whole nation disaffected, and in apprehension. . . .

18th September. I went to London, where I found the Court in the utmost consternation on report of the Prince of Orange's landing; which put Whitehall into so panic a fear, that I could hardly believe it possible to find such a change.

Writs were issued in order to a Parliament, and a declaration to back the good order of elections, with great professions of maintaining the Church of England, but without giving any sort of satisfaction to the people, who showed their high discontent at several things in the Government.

30th. The Court in so extraordinary a consternation, on assurance of the Prince of Orange's intention to land, that the writs sent forth for a Parliament were recalled. . . .

7th October. . . . Hourly expectation of the Prince of Orange's invasion heightened to that degree, that his Majesty thought fit to abrogate the Commission for the dispensing Power (but retaining his own right still to dispense with all laws) and restore the ejected Fellows of Magdalen College, Oxford. In the mean time, he called over 5,000 Irish, and 4,000 Scots, and continued to remove Protestants and put in Papists at Portsmouth and other places of trust, and retained the Jesuits about him, increasing the universal discontent. It brought people to so desperate a pass, that they seemed passionately to long for and desire the landing of that Prince, whom they looked on to be their deliverer from Popish tyranny, praying incessantly for an east wind, which was said to be the only hindrance of his expedition with a numerous army ready to make a descent. To such a strange temper, and unheard-of in former times, was this poor nation reduced, and of which I was an eyewitness. The apprehension was (and with reason) that his Majesty's forces

would neither at land nor sea oppose them with that vigour requisite to repel invaders.

The late imprisoned Bishops were now called to reconcile matters, and the Jesuits hard at work to foment confusion among the Protestants by their usual tricks. A letter was sent to the Archbishop of Canterbury, informing him, from good hands, of what was contriving by them. A paper of what the Bishops advised his Majesty was published. The Bishops were enjoined to prepare a form of prayer against the feared invasion. A pardon published. Soldiers and mariners daily pressed.

14th. The King's Birthday. No guns from the Tower as usual. The sun eclipsed at its rising. This day signal for the victory of William the Conqueror against Harold, near Battel, in Sussex. The wind, which had been hitherto west, was east all this day. Wonderful expectation of the Dutch fleet. Public prayers ordered to be read in the churches against invasion.

28th. A tumult in London on the rabble demolishing a Popish chapel that had been set up in the City.

29th. Lady Sunderland acquainted me with his Majesty's taking away the Seals from Lord Sunderland, and of her being with the Queen to intercede for him. It is conceived that he had of late grown remiss in pursuing the interest of the Jesuitical counsels; some reported one thing, some another; but there was doubtless some secret betrayed, which time may discover.

There was a Council called, to which were summoned the Archbishop of Canterbury, the Judges, the Lord Mayor, &c. The Queen Dowager, and all the ladies and lords who were present at the Queen Consort's labour, were to give their testimony upon oath of the Prince of Wales's birth, recorded both at the Council-Board and at the Chancery a day or two after. This procedure was censured by some as below his Majesty to condescend to, on the talk of the people. It was remarkable that on this occasion the Archbishop, Marquis of Halifax, the Earls of Clarendon and Nottingham, refused to sit at the Council-table amongst Papists, and their bold telling his Majesty that whatever was done whilst such sat amongst them was unlawful and incurred *praemunire*;[1]—at least, if what I heard be true. . . .

1st November. Dined with Lord Preston, with other company, at Sir Stephen Fox's. Continual alarms of the Prince of Orange, but no certainty. Reports of his great losses of horse in the storm, but without any assurance. A man was taken with divers papers and printed manifestoes, and carried to Newgate, after examination at the Cabinet-Council. There was likewise a Declaration of the States for satisfaction of all Public Ministers at the Hague, except to the English and the French. There was in that of the Prince's an expression, as if the Lords both Spiritual and Temporal had invited him over, with a deduction of the causes of his enterprise. This made his Majesty convene my Lord of Canterbury and the other Bishops now in town, to give an account of what was in the manifesto, and to enjoin them to clear themselves by some public writing of this disloyal charge. . . .

4th. Fresh reports of the Prince being landed somewhere about Portsmouth, or the Isle of Wight, whereas it was thought it would have been northward. The Court in great hurry.

5th. I went to London; heard the news of the Prince having landed at Torbay, coming with a fleet of near 700 sail, passing through the Channel with so favourable a wind, that our navy could not intercept, or molest them. This put the King and Court into great consternation, they were now employed in forming an army to stop their further progress, for they were got into Exeter, and the season and ways very improper for his Majesty's forces to march so great a distance.

The Archbishop of Canterbury and some

[1] *Praemunire* refers to the fourteenth century law against sending legislative and judicial appeals to the papal court at Rome. The Council here felt that the mere presence of papists constituted a breach of that law. [Editor's note]

few of the other Bishops and Lords in London, were sent for to Whitehall, and required to set forth their abhorrence of this invasion. They assured his Majesty they had never invited any of the Prince's party, or were in the least privy to it, and would be ready to show all testimony of their loyalty; but, as to a public declaration, being so few, they desired that his Majesty would call the rest of their brethren and Peers, that they might consult what was fit to be done on this occasion, not thinking it right to publish anything without them, and till they had themselves seen the Prince's Manifesto, in which it was pretended he was invited in by the Lords Spiritual and Temporal. This did not please the King; so they departed.

A Declaration was published, prohibiting all persons to see or read the Prince's Manifesto, in which was set forth at large the cause of his expedition, as there had been one before from the States.

These are the beginnings of sorrow, unless God in His mercy prevent it by some happy reconciliation of all dissensions among us. This, in all likelihood, nothing can effect except a free Parliament; but this we cannot hope to see, whilst there are any forces on either side. . . .

14th. The Prince increases every day in force. Several Lords go in to him. Lord Cornbury carries some regiments, and marches to Honiton, the Prince's headquarters. The City of London in disorder; the rabble pulled down the nunnery newly bought by the Papists of Lord Berkeley, at St. John's. The Queen prepares to go to Portsmouth for safety, to attend the issue of this commotion, which has a dreadful aspect.

18th. It was now a very hard frost. The King goes to Salisbury to rendezvous the army, and return to London. Lord Delamere appears for the Prince in Cheshire. The nobility meet in Yorkshire. The Archbishop of Canterbury and some Bishops, and such Peers as were in London, address his Majesty to call a Parliament. . . .

2nd December. Dr. Tenison preached at

St. Martin's on Psalm xxxvi. 5, 6, 7, concerning Providence. I received the blessed Sacrament. Afterwards, visited my Lord Godolphin, then going with the Marquis of Halifax and Earl of Nottingham as Commissioners to the Prince of Orange; he told me they had little power. Plymouth declared for the Prince. Bath, York, Hull, Bristol, and all the eminent nobility and persons of quality through England, declare for the Protestant religion and laws, and go to meet the Prince, who every day sets forth new Declarations against the Papists. The great favourites at Court, Priests and Jesuits, fly or abscond. Every thing, till now concealed, flies abroad in public print, and is cried about the streets. Expectation of the Prince coming to Oxford. The Prince of Wales and great treasure sent privily to Portsmouth, the Earl of Dover being Governor. Address from the Fleet not grateful to his Majesty. The Papists in offices lay down their commissions, and fly. Universal consternation amongst them; it looks like a revolution. . . .

9th. Lord Sunderland meditates flight. The rabble demolished all Popish chapels, and several Papist lords' and gentlemen's houses, especially that of the Spanish Ambassador, which they pillaged, and burnt his library.

13th. The King flies to sea, puts in at Feversham for ballast; is rudely treated by the people; comes back to Whitehall.

The Prince of Orange is advanced to Windsor, is invited by the King to St. James's, the messenger sent was the Earl of Feversham, the General of the Forces, who going without trumpet, or passport, is detained prisoner by the Prince, who accepts the invitation, but requires his Majesty to retire to some distant place, that his own guards may be quartered about the Palace and City. This is taken heinously, and the King goes privately to Rochester; is persuaded to come back; comes on the Sunday; goes to mass, and dines in public, a Jesuit saying grace (I was present).

17th. That night was a Council; his Majesty refuses to assent to all the proposals; goes away again to Rochester.

18th. I saw the King take barge to Gravesend at twelve o'clock—a sad sight! The Prince comes to St. James's, and fills Whitehall with Dutch guards. A Council of Peers meet about an expedient to call a Parliament; adjourn to the House of Lords. The Chancellor, Earl of Peterborough, and divers others taken. The Earl of Sunderland flies; Sir Edward Hales, Walker, and others, taken and secured.

All the world go to see the Prince at St. James's, where there is a great Court. There I saw him, and several of my acquaintance who came over with him. He is very stately, serious, and reserved. The English soldiers sent out of town to disband them; not well pleased.

24th. The King passes into France, whither the Queen and child were gone a few days before.

26th. The Peers and such Commoners as were members of the Parliament at Oxford, being the last of Charles II meeting, desire the Prince of Orange to take on him the disposal of the public revenue till a convention of Lords and Commons should meet in full body, appointed by his circular letters to the shires and boroughs, 22nd January. I had now quartered upon me a Lieutenant-Colonel and eight horses. . . .

1688-9. 15th January. I visited the Archbishop of Canterbury, where I found the Bishops of St. Asaph, Ely, Bath and Wells, Peterborough, and Chichester, the Earls of Aylesbury and Clarendon, Sir George Mackenzie Lord-Advocate of Scotland, and then came in a Scotch Archbishop, &c. After prayers and dinner, divers serious matters were discoursed, concerning the present state of the Public, and sorry I was to find there was as yet no accord in the judgments of those of the Lords and Commons who were to convene; some would have the Princess made Queen without any more dispute, others were for a Regency; there was a Tory party (then so called), who were for inviting his Majesty again upon conditions; and there were Republicans who would make the Prince of Orange like a Stadtholder. The Romanists were busy among these several parties to bring them into confusion: most for ambition or other interest, few for conscience and moderate resolutions. I found nothing of all this in this assembly of Bishops, who were pleased to admit me into their discourses; they were all for a Regency, thereby to salve their oaths, and so all public matters to proceed in his Majesty's name, by that to facilitate the calling of a Parliament, according to the laws in being. Such was the result of this meeting. . . .

The great convention being assembled the day before, falling upon the question about the Government, resolved that King James having by the advice of the Jesuits and other wicked persons endeavoured to subvert the laws of Church and State, and deserted the kingdom, carrying away the seals, &c., without any care for the management of the government, had by demise abdicated himself and wholly vacated his right; they did therefore desire the Lords' concurrence to their vote, to place the crown on the next heir, the Prince of Orange, for his life, then to the Princess, his wife, and if she died without issue, to the Princess of Denmark, and she failing, to the heirs of the Prince, excluding forever all possibility of admitting a Roman Catholic. . . .

29th. The votes of the House of Commons being carried up by Mr. Hampden, their chairman, to the Lords, I got a station by the Prince's lodgings at the door of the lobby to the House, and heard much of the debate, which lasted very long. Lord Derby was in the chair (for the House was resolved into a grand committee of the whole House); after all had spoken, it came to the question, which was carried by three voices against a Regency, which 51 were for, 54 against; the minority alleging the danger of dethroning Kings, and scrupling many passages and expressions in the vote of the Commons, too long to set down particularly. Some were for sending to his Majesty with conditions: others that the King could do no wrong, and that the maladministration was chargeable on his ministers. There were not more than eight or nine bishops, and but two against the Regency; the archbishop was absent, and the clergy now began to change their note, both in pulpit and discourse, on their old passive obedience, so as people began to talk of the bishops being cast out of the House. In short, things tended to dissatisfaction on both sides; add to this, the morose temper of the Prince of Orange, who showed little countenance to the noblemen and others, who expected a more gracious and cheerful reception when they made their court. The English army also was not so in order, and firm to his interest, nor so weakened but that it might give interruption. Ireland was in an ill posture as well as Scotland. Nothing was yet done towards a settlement. God of His infinite mercy compose these things, that we may be at last a Nation and a Church under some fixed and sober establishment. . . .

6th February. . . . The Convention of the Lords and Commons now declare the Prince and Princess of Orange King and Queen of England, France, and Ireland (Scotland being an independent kingdom), the Prince and Princess being to enjoy it jointly during their lives; but the executive authority to be vested in the Prince during life, though all proceedings to run in both names, and that it should descend to their issue, and for want of such, to the Princess Anne of Denmark and her issue, and in want of such, to the heirs of the body of the Prince, if he survive, and that failing, to devolve to the Parliament, as they should think fit. These produced a conference with the Lords, when also there was presented heads of such new laws as were to be enacted. It is thought on these conditions they will be proclaimed.

There was much contest about the King's abdication, and whether he had vacated the government. The Earl of Nottingham and about twenty Lords, and many Bishops, entered their protests, but the concurrence was great against them.

The Princess hourly expected. Forces sending to Ireland, that kingdom being in great danger by the Earl of Tyrconnel's army, and expectations from France coming to assist them, but that King was busy in invading Flanders, and encountering the German Princes. It is likely that this will be the most remarkable summer for action, which has happened in many years.

21st. . . . I saw the *new Queen* and *King* proclaimed the very next day after her coming to Whitehall, Wednesday, 13th February, with great acclamation and general good reception. Bonfires, bells, guns, &c. It was believed that both, especially the Princess, would have showed some (seeming) reluctance at least, of assuming her father's Crown, and made some apology, testifying by her regret that he should by his mismanagement necessitate the Nation to so extraordinary a proceeding, which would have showed very handsomely to the world, and according to the character given of her piety; consonant also to her husband's first declaration, that there was no intention of deposing the King, but of succouring the Nation; but nothing of all this appeared; she came into Whitehall laughing and jolly, as to a wedding, so as to seem quite transported. She rose early the next morning, and in her undress, as it was reported, before her women were up, went about from room to room to see the convenience of Whitehall; lay in the same bed and apartment where the late Queen lay, and within a night or two sat down to play at basset, as the Queen her predecessor used to do. She smiled upon and talked to everybody, so that no change seemed to have taken place at Court since her last going away, save that infinite crowds of people thronged to see her, and that she

went to our prayers. This carriage was censured by many. She seems to be of a good nature, and that she takes nothing to heart: whilst the Prince her husband has a thoughtful countenance, is wonderful serious and silent, and seems to treat all persons alike gravely, and to be very intent on affairs: Holland, Ireland, and France calling for his care.

Divers Bishops and Noblemen are not at all satisfied with this so sudden assumption of the Crown, without any previous sending, and offering some conditions to the absent King; or, on his not returning, or not assenting to those conditions, to have proclaimed him Regent; but the major part of both Houses prevailed to make them King and Queen immediately, and a crown was tempting. . . .

The Archbishop of Canterbury and some of the rest, on scruple of conscience and to salve the oaths they had taken, entered their protests and hung off, especially the Archbishop, who had not all this while so much as appeared out of Lambeth. This occasioned the wonder of many who observed with what zeal they contributed to the Prince's expedition, and all the while also rejecting any proposals of sending again to the absent King; that they should now raise scruples, and such as created much division among the people, greatly rejoicing the old courtiers, and especially the Papists.

Another objection was, the invalidity of what was done by a Convention only, and the as yet unabrogated laws; this drew them to make themselves on the 22nd [February] a Parliament, the new King passing the Act with the crown on his head. The lawyers disputed, but necessity prevailed, the Government requiring a speedy settlement.

Revolutionary Propaganda in the Midst of Battle

GILBERT BURNET

Gilbert Burnet, a disputatious Scotsman, left his native land and his first career in 1673 to climb into high church circles in England. He is best known for his *History of the Reformation*, written during Charles II's reign, and *History of His Own Time*, published posthumously. The latter is an excellent eyewitness account of the later Stuart period. As one of the exiles in Holland, Burnet attached himself to William of Orange's cause, acting as advisor and propagandist in preparing for the invasion. He became Bishop of Salisbury in 1689 and, after years of devotion to these clerical duties, died in 1715. The following piece was written either immediately before or shortly after William landed in England.

THIS enquiry cannot be regularly made, but by taking in the first place, a true and full view of the nature of civil society, and more particularly of the nature of supreme power, whether it is lodged in one or more persons?

It is certain, That the Law of Nature has put no difference nor subordination among men, except it be that of children to parents, or of wives to their husbands; so that with relation to the Law of Nature, all men are born free; and this liberty must still be supposed entire, unless so far as it is limited by contracts, provisions, or laws. For a man can either bind himself to be a servant, or sell himself to be a slave, by which he becomes in the power of another, only so far as it was provided by the contract: since all that liberty which was not expressly given away, remains still entire: so that the plea for liberty always proves itself, unless it appears that it is given up or limited by any special agreement.

It is no less certain, that as the light of nature has planted in all men a natural principle of the love of life, and of a desire to preserve it; so the common principles of all religion agree in this, that God having set us in this world, we are bound to preserve that being, which he has given us, by all just and lawful ways. Now this duty of self-preservation is exerted in instances of two sorts; the one are, in the resisting of violent aggressors; the other are the taking of just revenges of those, who have invaded us so secretly, that we could not prevent them, and so violently that we could not resist them: In which cases the principle of self-preservation warrants us, both to recover what is our own, with just damages, and also to put such unjust persons out of a capacity of doing the like injuries any more, either to ourselves, or to any others. Now in these two instances of self-preservation, this difference is to be observed; that the first cannot be limited

From Gilbert Burnet, "An Enquiry into the Measures of Submission to the Supreme Authority," in his *Collection of Eighteen Papers, Relating to the Affairs in Church and State During the Reign of King James the Second* (London, 1689), pp. 119–132.

by any slow forms, since a pressing danger requires a vigorous repulse, and cannot admit of delays; whereas the second, of taking revenges, or reparations, is not of such haste, but that it may be brought under rules and forms.

The true and original notion of civil society and government, is, that it is a compromise made by such a body of men, by which they resign up the right of demanding reparations, either in the way of justice against one another, or in the way of war, against their neighbours; to such a single person, or to such a body of men as they think fit to trust with this. And in the management of this civil society, great distinction is to be made, between the power of making laws for the regulating the conduct of it, and the power of executing those laws: The supreme authority must still be supposed to be lodged with those who have the legislative power reserved to them, but not with those who have only the executive; which is plainly a trust, when it is separated from the legislative power; and all trusts, by their nature import, that those to whom they are given, are accountable, even though that it should not be expressly specified in the words of the trust itself.

It cannot be supposed, by the principles of natural religion, that God has authorized any one form of government, any other way than as the general rules of order, and of justice, oblige all men not to subvert constitutions, nor disturb the peace of mankind, or invade those rights with which the law may have vested some persons: for it is certain, that as private contracts lodg[e] or translate private rights; so the public laws can likewise lodg[e] such rights, prerogatives and revenues in those under whose protection they put themselves, and in such a manner, that they may come to have as good a title to these, as any private person can have to his property: so that it becomes an act of high injustice and violence to invade these: which is so far a greater sin than any such actions would be against a private person, as the public peace and order is preferable to all private con-siderations whatsoever. So that in truth, the principles of natural religion, give those that are in authority no power at all, but they do only secure them in the possession of that which is theirs by law. And as no considerations of religion can bind me to pay another more than I indeed owe him, but do only bind me more strictly to pay what I owe; so the considerations of religion do indeed bring subjects under stricter obligations to pay all due allegiance and submission to their princes, but they do not at all extend that allegiance further than the law carries it. And though a man has no divine right to his property, but has acquired it by human means, such as succession, or industry; yet he has a security for the enjoyment of it from a divine right: so though princes have no immediate warrants from heaven, either for their original titles, or for the extent of them, yet they are secured in the possession of them by the principles and rules of natural religion. . . .

It is certain, that God, as the Creator and Governour of the world, may set up whom he will to rule over other men: But this declaration of his will must be made evident by prophets, or other extraordinary men sent of him, who have some manifest proofs of the divine authority that is committed to them on such occasions, and upon such persons declaring the will of God in favour of any others, that declaration is to be submitted to and obeyed. But this pretense of a divine delegation, can be carried no further than to those who are thus expressly marked out, and is unjustly claimed by those who can prove no such declaration to have been ever made in favour of them, or their families. Nor does it appear reasonable to conclude from their being in possession, that it is the will of God that it should be so, this justifies all usurpers when they are successful.

The measures of power, and by consequence of obedience, must be taken from the express laws of any state of body of men, from the oaths that they swear, or from immemorial prescription, and a long possession, which both give a title, and in a long tract of time make a bad one become good, since prescription, when it passes the memory of man, and is not disputed by any other pretender, gives by the common sense of all men a just and good title: so upon the whole matter, the degrees of all civil authority are to be taken either from express laws, immemorial customs, or from particular oaths, which the subjects swear to their princes: this being still to be laid down for a principle, that in all the disputes between power and liberty, power must always be proved, but liberty proves itself; the one being founded only upon a positive law, and the other upon the Law of Nature. . . .

The main and great difficulty here, is, that though our government does indeed assert the liberty of the subject, yet there are many express laws made, that lodg[e] the militia singly in the king, that make it plainly unlawful, upon any pretense whatsoever, to take arms against the king, or any commissioned by him: And these laws have been put in the form of an oath, which all that have borne any employment, either in church or state, have sworn; and therefore those laws for the assuring our liberties, do indeed bind the king's conscience, and may affect his ministers; yet since it is a maxim of our law, that the king can do no wrong, these cannot be carried so far as to justify our taking arms against him, be the transgressions of laws ever so many and so manifest. And since this has been the constant doctrine of the Church of England, it will be a very heavy imputation on us, if it appears, that though we held those opinions, as long as the court and crown have favoured us, yet as soon as the court turns against us, we change our principles.

Here is the true difficulty of this whole matter, and therefore it ought to be exactly considered: 1. All general words how large soever, are still supposed to have a tacit exception and reserve in them, if the matter seems to require it. Children are commanded to obey their parents in all things:

Wives are declared by the Scripture, to be subject to their husband in all things, as the church is unto Christ: And yet how comprehensive soever these words may seem to be, there is still a reserve to be understood in them; and though by our form of marriage, the parties swear to one another till death them do part, yet few doubt but that this bond is dissolved by adultery, though it is not named: for odious things ought not to be suspected, and therefore not named upon such occasions: But when they fall out, they carry still their own force with them. 2. When there seems to be a contradiction between two articles in the constitution, we ought to examine which of the two is the most evident, and the most important, and so we ought to fix upon it, and then we must give such an accommodating sense to that which seems to contradict it, that so we may reconcile those together. Here then are two seeming contradictions in our constitution; The one is the public liberty of the nation; the other is the renouncing of all resistance, in case that were invaded. It is plain, that our liberty is only a thing that we enjoy at the king's discretion, and during his pleasure, if the other against all resistance is to be understood according to the utmost extent of the words. Therefore since the chief design of our whole law, and of all the several rules of our constitution, is to secure and maintain our liberty, we ought to lay that down for a conclusion, that it is both the most plain, and the most important of the two. And therefore the other article against resistance ought to be so softened, as that it do not destroy us. 3. Since it is by a law that resistance is condemned, we ought to understand it in such a sense, as that it does not destroy all other laws: And therefore the intent of this law must only relate to the *executive* power, which is in the king, and not to the *legislative*, in which we cannot suppose that our legislators, who made that law, intended to give up that, which we plainly see they resolved still to preserve entire, according to the ancient constitution. So then, the not resisting the king, can only be applied to the executive power, that so upon no pretense of ill administrations in the execution of the law, it should be lawful to resist him; but this cannot with any reason be extended to an invasion of the legislative power, or to a total subversion of the government. For it being plain, that the law did not design to lodg[e] that power in the king; it is also plain, that it did not intend to secure him in it, in case he should set about it. 4. The law mentioning the king, or those commissioned by him, shows plainly, that it only designed to secure the king in the executive power: for the word commission necessarily imports this, since if it is not according to law, it is no commission; and by consequence, those who act in virtue of it, are not commissionated by the king in the sense of the law. The king likewise imports a prince clothed by law with the regal prerogative; but if he goes to subvert the whole foundation of the government, he subverts that by which he himself has his power, and by consequence he annuls his own powers and then he ceases to be king, having endeavoured to destroy that upon which his own authority is founded. . . .

The next thing to be considered, is to see in fact, whether the foundations of this government have been struck at, and whether those errors that have been perhaps committed, are only such malversations [malpractices] as ought to be imputed only to human frailty, and to the ignorance, inadvertencies, or passions to which all princes may be subject, as well as other men. But this will best appear, if we consider what are the fundamental points of our government, and the chief securities that we have for our liberties.

The authority of the law is indeed all in one word, so that if the king pretends to a power to dispense with laws, there is nothing left upon which the subject can depend; and yet as if the dispensing power were not enough, if laws are wholly suspended for all time coming, this is plainly a repealing of them, when likewise the

men, in whose hands the administration of justice is put by law, such as judges and sheriffs, are allowed to tread all laws underfoot, even those that infer an incapacity to themselves if they violate them: this is such a breaking of the whole constitution, that we can no more have the administration of justice, so that it is really a dissolution of the government; since all trials, sentences, and the executions of them are become so many unlawful acts, that are null and void of themselves.

The next thing in our constitution, which secures to us our laws and liberties, is a free and lawful parliament. Now, not to mention the breach of the law of triennial parliaments, it being above three years since we had a session that enacted any law; methods have been taken, and are daily [being taken], that render this impossible. Parliaments ought to be chosen with an entire liberty, and without either force or preingagements: whereas if all men are required beforehand to enter into engagements, how they will vote if they are chosen themselves? or how they will give their voices in the electing of others? This is plainly such a preparation to a parliament, as would indeed make it no parliament, but a cabal, if one were chosen after all that corruption of persons who had preingaged themselves, and after the threatening and turning out of all persons out of employments who had refused to do it: And if there are such daily regulations made in the towns, that it is plain those who manage them, intend at last to put such a number of men in the corporations, as will certainly choose the persons who are recommended to them. But above all, if there are such a number of sheriffs and mayors made over England, by whom the elections must be conducted and returned, who are now under an incapacity by law, and so are no legal officers, and by consequence those elections that pass under their authority are null and void: If, I say, it is clear that things are brought to this, then the government is dissolved, because it is impossible to have a free and legal parliament in this state of things. If then both the authority of the law, and the constitution of the parliament are struck at and dissolved, here is a plain subversion of the whole government. But if we enter next into the particular branches of the government, we will find the like disorder among them all.

The Protestant religion, and the Church of England make a great article of our government, the latter being secured, not only of old by Magna Charta, but by many special laws made of late; and there are particular laws made in K. Charles the First, and the late King's time, securing them from all commissions that the king can raise for judging or censuring them. If then in opposition to this, a court [of Ecclesiastical Commission] so condemned is erected, which proceeds to judg[e] and censure the clergy, and even to disseise [dispossess unlawfully] them of their freeholds, without so much as the form of a trial, though this is the most indispensible law of all those that secure the property of England; and if the king pretends that he can require the clergy to publish all his arbitrary declarations, and in particular one that strikes at their whole settlement, and has ordered process to be begun against all that disobeyed this illegal warrant; and has treated so great a number of the bishops as criminals, only for representing to him the reasons of their not obeying him. If likewise the king is not satisfied to profess his own religion openly, though even that is contrary to law, but has sent ambassadors to Rome, and received nuncio's from thence, which is plainly treason by law; If likewise many popish churches and chapels have been publicly opened; if several colleges of Jesuits have been set up in divers parts of the nation, and one of the Order has been made a privy counsellor, and a principal minister of state: And if papists, and even those who turn to that religion, though declared traitors by law, are brought into all the chief employments, both military and civil; then it is plain, that all the rights of the Church of England, and the whole establishment of the Protestant religion are struck at, and designed to be overturned; since all these things, as they are notoriously illegal, so they evidently demonstrate, that the great design of them all, is the rooting out of this pestilent heresy, in their stile, I mean, the Protestant religion.

In the next place, If in the whole course of justice, it is visible that there is a constant practicing upon the judges, that they are turned out upon their varying from the intentions of the court; and if men of no reputation nor abilities are put in their places; if an army is kept up in time of peace, and men who withdraw from that illegal service, are hanged up as criminals, without any colour of law, which by consequence are so many murders; and if the soldiery are connived at and encouraged in the most enormous crimes, that so they may be thereby prepared to commit greater ones, and from single rapes and murders proceed to a rape upon all our liberties, and a destruction of the nation: If, I say, all these things are true in fact; then it is plain, that there is such a dissolution of the government made, that there is not any one part of it left sound and entire: And if all these things are done now, it is easy to imagine what may be expected, when arbitrary power, that spares no man, and popery that spares no heretic, are finally established: Then we may look for nothing but gabelles, tailles, impositions, benevolences, and all sorts of illegal taxes; as from the other we may expect burning, massacres, and inquisitions. In what is doing in Scotland, we may gather what is to be expected in England; where the king has over and over again declared, that he is vested with an absolute power, to which all are bound to obey without reserve, and has upon that annulled almost all the acts of parliament that passed in K. James I minority, though they were ratified by himself when he came to be of age, and were confirmed by all the subsequent kings, not excepting the present. We must then conclude from thence, what is resolved on here in England, and what will be put in execution as soon as it is thought that the times can bear it. When likewise the whole settlement of Ireland is shaken, and the army that was raised, and is maintained by taxes that were given for an army of English Protestants, to secure them from a new massacre by the Irish papists, is now all filled with Irish papists, as well as almost all the other employments; it is plain, that not only all the British Protestants inhabiting that island, are in daily danger of being butchered a second time, but that the Crown of England is in danger of losing that island, it being now put wholly into the hands and power of the native Irish, who as they formerly offered themselves up sometimes to the Crown of Spain, sometimes to the Pope, and once to the Duke of Lorrain, so are they perhaps at this present treating with another court for the sale and surrender of the island, and for the massacre of the English in it.

If thus all the several branches of our constitution are dissolved, it might be at least expected that one part should be left entire, and that is the regal dignity. And yet even that is prostituted, when we see a young child put in the reversion of it, and pretended to be the Prince of Wales: concerning whose being born of the Queen, there appear to be not only no certain proofs, but there are all the presumptions that can possibly be imagined to the contrary. No proofs were ever given, either to the Princess of Denmark, or to any other Protestant ladies, in whom we ought to repose any confidence, that the Queen was ever with child; that whole matter being managed with so much mysteriousness, that there were violent and public suspicions of it before the birth. But the whole contrivance of the birth, the sending away the Princess of Denmark, the sudden shortening of the reckoning, the Queen's sudden going to St. James's, her no less sudden pretended delivery; the hurrying the child into another room without showing it to those present, and without their hearing it cry; and the mysterious conduct of all since that time; no satisfaction being given to the Princess of Denmark upon her return from the bath, nor to any other Protestant ladies, of the Queen's having been really brought to bed. These are all such evident indications of a base imposture in this matter, that as the nation has the justest reason in the world to doubt of it, so they have all possible reason to be at no quiet till they see a legal and free parliament assembled, which may impartially, and without either fear or corruption, examine that whole matter.

If all these matters are true in fact, then I suppose no man will doubt, that the whole foundations of this government, and all the most sacred parts of it, are overturned. And as to the truth of all these suppositions, that is left to every Englishman's judgment and sense.

The Revolution as Immoral, Illegal, and Anti-monarchical

THE JACOBITES

This pamphlet, like most Jacobite works, is anonymous. Anonymity was a device resorted to frequently to forestall charges of sedition or libel. The pamphlet is representative of many, expressing the ultra-legalism of the Jacobite movement and the bitterness caused by the events of 1688–89. The author insists that only a firm adherence to the laws of succession and non-resistance can restore the rule of law in England. Note that "K. J." and "K. W." refer to King James and King William; and that "P. of O." means the Prince of Orange (William).

I F it be true that interest is often mistaken, though it never lie, and that standers-by sometimes see more than gamesters, though they do not understand the game so well, it may not be false that the politic drivers of our late revolution in England (who, 'tis to be feared, have too many of them designed their private interest at least as much as that of the public), have mistaken their way to both, and that one who has been no more than an indifferent looker-on, and who pretends not to be clearer sighted than others, has observed some things which the abler gamesters have not been aware of. Whether it be so or not, who pleases to read the following observations may judge. I will preface no more to him, whoever he be, than that if he examine them, as they have done the matter of fact on both sides, without prejudice to any, he will judge the better; and that since my kindness for my friends and country is the only motive I can have to expose my thoughts of this nature, he will be very unkind if he does not forgive what he does not approve.

First Observation. That though religion in the contrivance of this turn was called upon at first to serve the turn of interest, as it has ever been put to do in changes of this kind, and did sanctify a little while the pride and ambition of private men, with the name of Blessed Reformation, and made saints among the ignorant people of the worthy gentlemen so qualified, it has nevertheless been treated by them with less ceremony, than has been shown it before on such occasions. That mask was immediately thrown off here, and interest appeared bare-faced in everybody's mouth from the very beginning. . . . In short, men of war, men of law, men of gospel, men of all kinds, professed plainly to stand up for their liberty and property against their king; and that not so much by covering them, under the defense of their religion, as by discovering their religion was to defend them. So that though religion was advanced sometimes to lead up the common people, and marched along with liberty and property at the head of parties and pamphlets, when there was occasion

From "Observations upon the Late Revolution in England," in *A Collection of Scarce and Valuable Tracts* [Somers Tracts] (London, 1813), vol. X, pp. 336–348.

to appear in public, it was plain that my lords and gentlemen had no other use of it, than to gull the commonalty; and that the profits and preferments of the government, to which the laws and possession gave them a title, were the things they would never part with, if any other king, or if no king, would preserve them to them.

Second Observation. That their redeemer, the P. of O., had the same occasion, and made just the same use of religion as his religiously aggrieved inviters and assisters into England; his declaration setting forth the deep sense and concern he had for it, as plainly as they could speak and write theirs. . . . [Furthermore,] whoever observes that the shoe pinches chiefly in the point of the Prince of Wales, who put the Prince of Orange by [out of] his hopes of succession, even more if it were true, than if it were fictitious, and that therefore . . . it was absolutely necessary to make him appear fictitious if possible; and whoever considers these other proceedings of the Prince of Orange upon all occasions; the trouble he gave himself of coming over into England about ten years ago, on purpose to help forward the Bill of Exclusion against the Duke of York; his entering into a conspiracy (which is averred from the mouth of one trusted by himself at the very time) for . . . deposing K. Ch. II.; his unwearied diligence in thwarting every thing K. C. or K. J. had a mind to have done by their own subjects; his great goodness in providing well for all those persons, who, for some goodness or other, had incurred their displeasure, and were banished or proclaimed traitors by those two kings; his generosity in sending and making use of the Duke of Monmouth, like foot of whelp, to burn his paws with setting up for king in England, without men, money, or arms; his courage afterwards, so much extolled, in coming himself, when, being rid of Monmouth's pretensions, he had the consent of the greatest part of the people and army of England, and knew he was not to strike any other kind of stroke for it than such

. . . as he gave with his whip on a gentleman's shoulders at Newmarket, for riding before him, wittily enough observed then, to be the first he struck for the kingdom; his great care of K. J. when he was betrayed by his own army, in sending him a Dutch guard to Whitehall at eleven o'clock at night, without his knowing anything of it; . . . his constant and firm adherence, after the king's departure, to his declaration (the confidence of which had drawn in all the people to him;) first, in his calling a free and legal parliament, than which he declares to have no other design; secondly, in the particular care he took for electing to his parliament, called the Convention, all true churchmen, all such as had been discountenanced, or brow-beaten before, in the way of outlawries, or so, by King Charles the Second, or King James; all such as could possibly be found, who had any hand of their own, or relation to those who had, in bringing his grandfather King Charles the First to condign punishment; and, thirdly, in his not suffering any business of the kingdom to come before or be thought of, by his honourable convention; not so much as his dearly beloved consort the princess, who, though she was graciously mentioned in his declaration, to have so great an interest in this matter, and such a right as all the world knows, to the succession of the crown, was not then permitted to come into England, till they had altered the fundamental constitution of the government, and made him king in his own right; his transubstantiating, (as it has been called) when he was king, the same convention into a parliament, without writs or new elections, lest he should not get the people, who had been deceived by their conventionary members doing what they never dreamed of in making him king, to choose such parliament men as would serve the turns he had to come hereafter; . . . his filling all places of trust and profit throughout the kingdom, as far as could be found, with persons of the church of England, and of good life and conversation; his sending out of England even for Mr. Ludlow, one of the regicides of his grandfather, attainted and condemned by act of parliament for hanging up without a trial, to be advised with, if not preferred in the government here; his free disinterested submission of this kingdom's business to this free parliament, without any of those tricks as were played by former kings to influence or bias the members, as appears by its being so well an officered parliament, as it has been observed to be in the House of Commons itself; by the lords' sons he has called up, and the new peers he has created, by his sending his own Bentinck, whom he never parts with, when he has no particular interest driving elsewhere, out of his closet, to vote for Mr. Oats's being a good evidence again; . . . his religious way of taking and keeping coronation oaths in England, to defend episcopacy, and the church of England, as established by law; for the special performance of which, all England sees itself obliged to his weak endeavours; in Scotland to abolish episcopacy, root and branch, and to establish a church more conformable to the word of God, for the godly performance of which, all Scotland see no church at all. To conclude, upon this whole matter, it is observed, that his Dutch highness, as well as his English factors, consulted his private interest and ambition in the redemption he brought to England, at least as much as he did the good of religion, or the interest of the kingdom.

*   *   *

Fourth Observation. That setting aside the question, whether the proceedings of the people of England have been just or lawful, it is observed that what they have done, is directly against their dearly beloved and espoused interest, and worse for themselves, in the same kind, than any inconveniences King James could have brought them under; that is to say, that those very inconveniences, of what kind soever they were, which they apprehended from him, (and everybody knows they were not more than apprehended) are actually insupportable under this change of government already, and that they will grow worse and worse still, without other remedy than restoring him again; which will appear best by comparing what we feared then with what we feel now. . . .

. . . we feared for our laws, not so much I believe for what was done, as for the manner of doing it, for I am persuaded a good part of what King James did might have been done for him in a legal way, and with the consent of the people; but when we saw him assume a dispensing power, not vested in him by law, we were sensible that the same power which overruled one law, might over-rule another, and all, and feared the pernicious example: This, I think, was the case and the disease. The antidote now which we have taken against the poison of this bad example, is it not an example as bad, or worse, and our remedy against one illegal power, which we have pulled down, a setting up another altogether as illegal?

For the law acknowledges not for a legal parliament, any number of men, who are strong enough, a legal call; no, though they convene in the parliament-house, and vote themselves a parliament, nor that man for a king, whom the law places not in the throne. Unriddle me now, who can, in what an illegal dispensing power was more dangerous to our laws, than an illegal enactive, or an illegal executive power is; or in what the abdicated example of K. J. to dispense with some laws, was worse than the example set up now, by which any number of men who are strong enough, may assume an absolute power to dispose of all our laws, our religion, our bodies, consciences, and purses as they please, with no more ceremony than the formality of a transubstantiating vote. A liberty- and property-defending army of Englishmen, has done little less within the memory of man, and if our Dutch redeemers should take it for the fashion of the country, and to complete our redemption, set up for the parliament of England, which way can we plead our laws in bar to them, which we have over-ruled already ourselves? In short, illegality is always illegality, and if that were the intolerable pernicious thing before, it is so much the more intolerable now, by how much a legislative illegality is more pernicious than a dispensative one, and an usurped executive power more dangerous than a legal one; and yet the wisdom of our fears has drank down one, as a destructive disturbing, and the other, as a healing settling draught. I am far enough from kindness to either, but I will say for the destructive one, that it has been, at least, the more modest of the two, for it only made bold with a single superstructure, by dispensing with the test-act, without which our government had stood many a fair age, and that too with a pretense on its side of its being law, in the interval of parliament, and of referring it to a parliament when it met; whereas our settling illegality has fallen confidently upon the very foundations of our constitution, and pulled them quite away. The English government has hitherto stood upon these fundamental maxims, that the king never dies, and that all authority is derived from him. For our wise ancestors were so sensible of the ruinous consequences of interregnums, elections, seditions, and saw so well that nothing could prevent them but a legal king always in being, that they would not allow to death itself, with all its irresistible power over the man, any power over the king, but made the same moment which received the last breath of the man breathe his regal power into the next of blood; and then placing the fountain of all authority in this immortal king, stopped up forever all pretending streams of sedition. By this it was made impossible, for any pretense to cheat or hinder the people from distinguishing the seditious, which they were to avoid, from the just power which they were to obey, there being no more to do, but to ask which flowed from that fountain which they had contrived should always run. Now we have introduced vacant thrones, filling them as pleasure or humour, not as blood directs, and a new power over our fundamentals themselves, not derived from the old only fountain; and now to make the hinges straight, upon

which how much soever they swayed before by dispensing, our government still moved, we have knocked them quite off. I will not be the melancholy prophet to foretell what will be the consequence, but leave every one to guess, who will reflect what they have seen and felt in one year's time. . . .

*   *   *

Sixth   Observation. That though we thought to make our court to our new king by deserting our old, as we are generally an honest, upright people, our consciences possibly, if they were not ashamed to speak, could tell strange stories of the self-denial this compliment cost us, and the hard shifts and pains many of us made, and took to mortify the struggling rebellion of nature against that which we unnaturally hurried ourselves into against our king. And for getting the better of ourselves, for the fruits of this glorious victory, our ears tell us every day, that cowardice and treachery (reproaches heretofore unusual to Englishmen) fly in our faces from the mouths of our conquerors, from such of them at least as cannot be hindered from saying what they think, which is enough to instruct us what the reserved rest have to say, whose time it is not yet to speak their thoughts. Our eyes tell us, that no Englishman is trusted in anything, no not those who for form-sake sit in places of trust, for as our English estates are often settled in trust, our English trust itself is in trust now; the fine titles worn by our ministers and privy-counsellors of England being nothing but gay liveries, to make them show the handsomer tools to finish up the work cut out by Dutchmen in the closet. And our reason will tell us we cannot complain, nor expect it ever should be otherwise. For no wise prince will trust a man whom he has cause to suspect will not be true to him; and our K. W. cannot forget that he was not born in England, that he did not inherit the crown, that he cannot reign without wars and taxes: and that therefore he cannot (though he would never so fain) securely count upon those men, whereof every one who presents himself for employment, must of necessity come with this speech in his mouth: You, sir, are king *de facto,* and may be sure of me; for I am just come from being false to a king *de facto,* and *de jure* both, who was my countryman, besides, twenty to one, my particular benefactor, and whose reign was a reign of peace and plenty. Our compliment therefore has put an inevitable necessity upon our new king, never to trust us to counsel or fight for ourselves, but under a sure guard, and to furnish himself with store of foreign heads and hands, to carry on the interest of England; at which we are neither to wonder nor complain, for necessity has no law.

Seventh Observation. That all this mischief cannot follow only (as some would have, and do infer) from K. James's going away, called Abdication; for though abdication is a hard word, which I will not pretend to understand, because my dictionary does not, I am sure it means not what his going away plainly was, trying to escape a foreseen restraint, and escaping at last an actual one. But I guess what they would have meant by it is, that K. James when he went away, ceased to be K. some way or other, which yet was neither giving away out of liberality, nor selling for money, nor losing his crown by chance, nor forfeiting, nor surrendering, nor dying. But what unintelligible way soever it were, the moment in which he ceased to be king (according to our constitution) some other was king; in which case we had no more to do but to let our government move upon the old sure wheels, and our happiness would have gone on along with it under the new king, whom God and nature, and the law of England, have always in readiness for us when the old fails. So that let abdicating signify what it will, I see no necessity of shaming ourselves with the imputation of a faithless, simple people, neither to be trusted by any king, nor so much as with our own concerns and interest: No necessity of for-

eigners, and the calamities they must bring along with them: None of subverting the foundation of our constitution, and crushing ourselves with the falling building. It had been but keeping the laws, and they would have kept us. But as we have handled the matter, with our anteponing and postponing, we have brought the government of England to the domineering of a [mob], with all their whimsies, and all their violence, with only a more formal outside: for there is no such thing as a government left, to which anybody is obliged to submit for any reason but fear: No such thing as law, which has been, or can be legally made or executed; and let a man have deserved to have been condemned never so much the last year, he needs his pardon who condemned him. In short, we are absolutely in the state of nature before society, where all the power which one man had over another was his greater strength, and all authority violence. 'Tis by violence K. W. calls conventions and parliaments; and violence is all the validity of their acts. They have no other authority than the laws which thieves make among themselves to rob the more methodically and safely; and we submit to both, for the same reason, fear of worse. Violence seizes our money and our liberty, and we yield to it, just as we suffer stronger highwaymen to bind us and take our purses. Were the just scales of the law in use, (for the dispensing with which in one particular we were in such frights before) every order now for a tax, every assessment, every collection, and perhaps (if necessity help us not off) every payment would weigh more than felony, downright treason: And what the men of might do to us, every one of us, who happens to be strong enough, may with as much right do to them.

Eighth Observation. To conclude: Here we are, and here we must be eternally, till we learn wit of a carter, and set the overturned cart on the wheels again; in plain terms, till we re-settle King James on his throne. The happiness of England depends upon a rightful king, we see it always went out with him, and 'tis in vain to hope it ever will, or can return without him. . . .

We may have a lawful government and true parliaments again, security of our religion, laws, and rights, and be once more the freemen we were born, re-enfranchized from wars and taxes; for all these things are waiters in ordinary, and return with the king of course. If any remnant of our former fears hangs still uneasy about us, he is not so far off, but a willing mind may have recourse to him, whither he has more than once invited us for that purpose, and be eased. And it is not now to be suspected, he will boggle at condescending to any thing that is reasonable in our fears, much less that we shall ever have reason to complain hereafter of non-performance. For as there is no security like interest, and he cannot but be sensible of it, who sees that not to keep his word, is not to keep his kingdom; if we have but wit enough to judge as the wise Romans did, even upon the suggestion of a conquered enemy, that a reasonable easy peace on both sides, is sincere and lasting; an unreasonable grating one on either side, of no longer durance than till the next opportunity for war, and so keep ourselves from grating unreasonably upon him; the wit of a burned child in him will set our hearts at rest for that matter: But have him we must on any terms, or be the most wretched nation under the sun: For the fire of war is kindled, which of necessity must otherwise consume us. . . . We live in an island, where, conversing only among ourselves, we are apt to think the world goes as the cry goes with us, and perceive not how abominably we stink in the nostrils of all mankind besides; not excepting the very Turks, nor our delivering masters themselves, for the glory of wearing whose chains we have made ourselves so wretchedly despicable. Not to flatter ourselves, all Europe loaths a nation which, having murdered one king, is now murdering another, and that not by a ragged [mob] whose unthinking fury starts more excusably into horrid crimes,

but by a [mob] of another make, a [mob] of honour dressed up in the wisdom and devotion of the nation; a thinking godly [mob], which kills in cool blood, and fasts and prays to sanctify the murders. To be plain, all Europe hates our hypocrisy, who, pretending zeal for the protestant religion, are all the while worse than the very worst of papists.

Alas! that England should for our sakes bid fair to lose its old name, and be known hereafter by the name of the barbarous, the king-killing country; and our religion the faithless, the hypocritical religion!

But it is time to end, and I will, if I can, end with demonstration. It is demonstration that, unless we recover our old constitution by consent, we must, besides the intermediate miseries, sink at last under arbitrary power. It may be monarchical, and it may be republican. But arbitrary it must be, if we suffer it to come either to a conquest of King William, or King James, or to a commonwealth; which, by the way, would be the worst of all; we can at least complain under an arbitrary prince, and the shame and vexation of just complaints is some check to him, let him be never so absolute. Under a commonwealth there is not so much as that poor ease; as imaginations of law or fancy, I know not whether, makes us do whatever our representatives do; no burthen can pass for oppression, nor complaint for just. For we oppress ourselves all the while, and must complain of ourselves, and whatever we suffer in reality, all is ease and liberty in imagination. But this is no place for the dispute betwixt monarchy and a commonwealth. It is enough that conquest makes a conqueror absolute; that nothing can be more arbitrary than a commonwealth must be, and that a weight weighs its weight however it be laid on. It is demonstration that we cannot recover our old constitution, without our old king. It stands upon right of blood, it fell with that right, and we may as soon build a castle in the air as think to rear and prop it again with our politic fancies. . . .

The Revolution as a Chance to Erect a Republic

THE REPUBLICANS

These two anonymous pamphlets represent part of the republican position during early 1689, at a time when no one knew in what direction the constitution would move. Obviously the authors wish, though not hopefully, that monarchy, if not finally abolished, will at least be heavily circumscribed by parliamentary privilege by the Convention. Notice the guarded tone of the pieces, probably caused by the knowledge that republican views were considered with far less favor than forty years earlier.

NOW IS THE TIME:
A SCHEME FOR A COMMONWEALTH

THE thing that offers itself in this great conjuncture is, to have a grand committee of Lords and Commons (forty at least from each house) to be as a privy council, or council of state, or governing senate.

It were to be wished, that twenty of each forty might be for life, and the other twenty biennial, ten going off every year; or half might be changed annually.

Each senator or counsellor to have for his salary maintenance one thousand pounds a year. This would be such an advancement to the nobility and gentry as England never saw. And the charge is a trifle. There is more spent in some monarchies upon hawks, hounds, and whores.

The prince to preside in this council or senate (or such person as he shall appoint in his stead) and to have ten votes at least. He must also be general and admiral; and must have such further powers, and such a maintenance or revenue, as his infinite merits require; but withall, such as are consistent with the government he designs for us. The prince's maintenance should equal, or exceed, that of all the senators put together.

All that are of this council, and all that hope to be (that is, all the considerable men of the nation) will by this means be firm to the prince. And so will those others who have the great privilege of choosing them, whereby they may have confidence in his administration. And this one thing will give the prince so strong an interest, that he needs fear no pretension that can be against him. It will be better than a standing army: The necessity whereof nothing can prevent but such a standing council.

The parliament to be chosen triennially, and to meet annually.

It is believed that such a constitution as this would effectually secure us (according to the prince's good intentions) from popery and tyranny. And the prince will be the glorious author of the Britannic liberty, as his grandfather was of the Belgian. The Genoese to this day adore the memory of Andrew Doria, who chose rather to make them a free state than to be their prince. Barely to change our master would but revive the feuds of York and Lancaster, and involve us in the like calamities.

From *Somers Tracts*, vol. X, pp. 197–202.

These things to continue but during the life of the king, and not to prejudice a protestant successor.

GOOD ADVICE BEFORE IT BE TOO LATE

Whereas we cannot but be made very apprehensive . . . lest the swaying part of the nation should be so much intent upon one thing as that others be neglected; or lest they be so taken up with putting the crown upon an head most deserving it, as that they forget what is to be done first; which is, the consideration of the constitution of the realm, and the declaring that constitution, before any person be admitted into actual regiment; it being common for those who look but on one thing to be too sudden. We therefore judge it meet, that this ensuing paper, which was in a few copies given to some members of the houses, for preventing that evil, should also be made public, to go abroad with such papers as those of the former nature: For as it is wise in a people, when they make any compact, whether with their rulers or others, that though they believe the party they deal with to be the best in the world, to treat with him for all that, and be as punctual upon the terms, to make all secure, as if they were dealing with the worst; so it is also honest for them, in seeking the good of their country, to deny self-interest, and to prefer the benefiting a nation before the magnifying any single person whatsoever.

The people of this nation are by birth a free people, who are born to a liberty of person and propriety in their goods and lands; and therefore England is rightly called a free state.

To understand the government, we must know that these two things are always to be distinguished, the Constitution and the Administration.

The constitution of a government does lie in the original agreement of the people, which they make between themselves, or with their intended governor or governors, before the government be set up, whether there be none before, or the former at an end.

When the people are in such a state, while there is no order of superiority or inferiority introduced, it is called a Community: When a ruler is chosen, so that there is a ruling and ruled part, it is a society, or called a Commonwealth.

Let us suppose a company of families, that having no dependence on one another, nor any one having power over the other, yet living near each other, do find it convenient to join together in a society, for mutual defense against some foreign enemy, or for the reaping several advantages which they shall receive by it. The heads or representatives of these families assembled, are to consider what is to be done in order to these ends.

Three things more especially they must consult upon;

1. What government (as to the sort or kind) is best for them?

2. Who shall be governor or governors?

3. And by what laws or rules they shall govern, who are entrusted with the supreme power?

And more particularly, in relation to what measure of it they will allow them to have over their persons and estates, to use them as they have occasion for the public good. For when they are yet free in both, the governor can have power so far, but no farther than they at first consent. Whatsoever reservations of liberty the people make in their agreement, these are to be looked upon as their rights by the laws of the constitution, and essential thereunto, and consequently inviolable by any of these governors whom they set up for the administration; the very laws of the administration being void, so far as they interfere with any of these of the constitution. . . .

Our government now, as constituted in order to this administration, is, we know, a mixed government. A government is known to be pure or mixed, by the placing the supreme authority. If the people place it singly in the king, or singly in the nobles, or singly in the people, then it is a mixed government, as ours is, where there are no laws in the administration made but by king, lords, and commons. . . .

The supreme power of the nation being placed in a parliament, which is a corporation of king, lords, and commons, that is, the supreme authority residing in king, lords, and commons, as one corporation, there does appear, at this conjuncture, a dissolution of the government, a dissolution manifestly as to the exercise of it. This appearance does arise from the opening of the last scene; for the king being now gone, gone from his people, and departing from his government, that one corporation (we speak of) is broke; so that there remains now no subject for that supreme authority; it being evident that a parliament, wherein an essential point of our constitution does consist, cannot now be assembled: And the providence of God itself hath extraordinarily determined our case. If a king dies he hath a successor, and the right devolves upon him; but whilst the king lives he hath no successor, and the right remaining in him and no other, and he being divided from his lords and commons, the subject of the supreme power, or this one corporation (whereof the king is a chief, essential and constituent part) does perfectly cease, and must necessarily cause a dissolution.

I choose not to found this upon what does more convince others, which comes to this account: The king, by his frequent malversation in the government, and rooted design of subverting our religious and civil rights, for the introduction of arbitrary power and popery, which being aggravated by such an endeavour, as the destroying that share in the government which every commoner hath that hath a right to choose his representative in parliament, by his garbling corporations, and so evacuating this liberty in effect; and by such an endeavour also as the exterminating his protestant subjects, seeing that religion which he would have introduced is such as, by the principles of it, if it comes into denomination, must do so to all heretics; and thereupon may he be looked on no longer as *Rex*, but *Hostis*, and *Hostis Publicus* [enemy of the people]: Besides, the subjecting us to a foreign jurisdiction, and the very changing the government, by that indefinite dispensing power over the laws as was carved to him by his judges, from regal to despotical, it is judged by them that he is fallen thereupon from his royal dignity; and that the universality thereby have warrant not only to defend themselves against him, but by virtue of that sanction, which is tacitly implied in the laws of the constitution, to proceed on to take the forfeiture he hath made of his government, and depose him: For it is a fond thing (think they) to imagine any laws without a sanction; and impossible there should be any other sanction in treaties between free nations, or between a free people, and the governor they set over themselves, than force to be used by the parties concerned; there being no third party on earth to appeal to in such cases.

However this be, it being taken for granted that the government is dissolved, and I suppose upon that preceding account, of the one corporation (I say) being broke, the supreme authority that lay before in the three as united in one, does escheat or fall to the community; who must therefore choose a new subject for that power; and it lies at their discretion to place it in what subject they please: They may lodge it in the lords and commons alone, without a king, if they think that government best; the matter lies altogether upon their agreement and consent. I suppose it most likely, that they will agree to place it again in a monarch, lords, and commons (the person only left at choice, and care had to prevent all danger of law in the case) according to the ancient constitution; though what man can know the mind of a nation, when once come together, if he knows his own mind?

There is one thing we have now opportunity to obtain, which we can never recover again if it be lost, and that is, what his highness the Prince of Orange hath made one of his two designs, the delivery of the people from slavery; which can never be done effectually and radically but upon this advantage. The delivering us from popery is contained in the settling our religion; and that, being a work of great length, is the business more properly of a parliament; but this is a thing must be done by the community, and consequently by those that are the representatives of it, a convention, so called (in regard to a higher capacity hereunto), and not a parliament; for that represents the people, not as in a community but as in a commonwealth, where there is *pars imperans* [majority], as well as *subdita* [minority], which now is not. A parliament makes laws for the administration, but the people, as in a community, make laws for the constitution.

I would therefore humbly offer it to the consideration of those, who shall meet as members of this convention, that, in order to the effect premised, they do but agree and pitch upon this one certain point of good polity, that where they place the supreme authority, they lay also the rights or properties of it; that is, the *Jura Majestatis* [the rights of majesty] (*majestas* being *maxima potestas* [the highest power]) altogether.

The rights of majesty, or the supreme power, are mainly these: The first is legislation, or making laws; and this undoubtedly lies in a parliament. The next is the power of raising arms, or armies, or the militia, the power of making peace and war, or power of the sword, which is necessary to maintain those laws. The third is a power over our estates, or the purse, or raising money, which must maintain the sword. A fourth is, the power of choosing magistrates to rule us according to these laws; such as judges and sheriffs, to name no other. A fifth is, the last appeal. Now, let but the power of the militia and choosing magistrates be laid where legislation is, and we shall be fundamentally delivered from all slavery forever in the nation.

If we be enslaved or oppressed by any prince for the time to come, it must be either by force or by injustice. We cannot be oppressed by force, because no forces then can be raised by him, but by a parliament. He cannot rule by an army, or by violence; for the militia is in the lords and commons as well as in him, and they will not let him do so: We cannot be oppressed with injustice; for the judges and officers entrusted with the execution of justice shall be chosen also by them, and they will look to that.

It is true, while no parliament sits, the king, by virtue of the executive power lying in him, may raise arms, and put in officers and magistrates as there is need; but both these are to be done under the control of the next parliament (which are therefore to sit often by ancient statutes), there being no war to be levied, nor magistrates confirmed, without their approbation.

Let us remember the state we are in, a state that puts the supreme power in the hands of the people, to place it as they will: and therefore to bound and limit it as they see fit for the public utility; and if they do it not now, the ages to come will have occasion to blame them forever. When the supreme power is upon the disposing, if they do not take this item as part of their proper work, "To bind the descent of it to a protestant," I shall blame them: But I shall do so much more, if, after the danger we have been in, of arbitrary domination and popery, by the king's raising arms, and putting judges in and out at his pleasure, they do not take more care of the supreme power, to lay it and its rights better together; especially seeing nothing can indeed be that in nature, which it is, without its properties. This is uniform (I must persist) to the nature of government, that where the supreme authority is, there must be its prerogatives; and where the chief or principal rights of it is, there should all the rest which depend upon and belong to it be placed also: Where legislation is lodged, there should the militia, there should the power of making judges, to name nothing more than serves my turn, be lodged also. It is this hath been the great declension, fault, or defect of our English commonwealth, that the people have suffered these rights of sovereignty to come to be divided, arising (we must conceive) from the administration, that is, maladministration: as appears, for example, in the militia, which, upon the fresh coming in of the late king, was, in two or three hot acts, declared now and ever to have been in the king; when both the assertion was gross flattery, and such acts void, as fundamentally repugnant to the constitution.

There is one difficulty to be thought on, and that is, the negative voice of the prince in his parliament. The lords and commons may agree upon some law for the public benefit, and the king alone may refuse to pass it. If he be obstinate this is a great evil, and might really make one think, it would be better therefore (for the preventing this inconvenience) to place the supreme power in lords and commons only, without a controller. Unto which may be added, the power of calling and dissolving parliaments at pleasure; by virtue whereof, our kings hitherto have pretended a power predominant over them. But forasmuch as these prerogatives may be disputed, and the negative voice hath been denied by many judicious men, who have pleaded the obligation of former princes to confirm those laws, *quas vulgus elegerit;* it is to be hoped that the wisdom of the nation will be able to find out some expedient or salve for this difficulty, and for more than that also: so long as they have the golden opportunity to bring a crown in one hand, with their terms or conditions in the other.

As for the several grievances that need redress, and many good things that are wanting to complete the happiness of our kingdom, there may be some foundation laid happily, or preparations made in order thereunto by this convention; but as belonging to the administration, and being matters of long debate, they are the work more properly of an ensuing parliament. Only let not the members of this present great assembly forget, that they having so unlimited a power, and the nation such an opportunity, which, as the secular games, they are never like to see but once, they are more strictly therefore bound in conscience, and in duty to their country, to neglect no kind of thing which they judge absolutely necessary to the public good. I care not if I commend three or four such particulars against the time to consultation, which shall be these: A regulation of Westminster-hall; a provision against buying or selling of offices; a register of estates; a freedom from persecution (by a bill for comprehension and indulgence) in the business of religion; a redemption of the chimney-money, which, bringing the king to be lord of every man's house, is against property; and an overbalance in the revenue is against the interest of the nation.

The Breviate being ended, we cannot but reflect upon the king; there being so much concern in the minds of many, about their allegiance to him, though he be gone: but such persons as these should look a little more to the bottom, that a people is not made for the king, but the king for the people; and though he be greater than them in some respects, yet, *quoad finem,* the people are always greater than him: that is, if the good of the one and the other stand in competition, there is no comparison but a nation is to be preferred before one man. If the being of them be inconsistent one with another, there is no doubt but it is better that a king cease, than that a whole nation should perish. . . .

The Revolution as an Act of Conquest

WILLIAM LLOYD

William Lloyd, Bishop of St. Asaph (not to be confused with the non-juring William Lloyd), was born in 1627. He was one of the strongest opponents of the court Jesuits in James II's reign and one of the Seven Bishops who refused to read James's second Declaration of Indulgence. The following work represents the justification of the Revolution from the High Church point of view which modified divine right theory, thus making it applicable to William's kingship. It was first delivered as a sermon before William and Mary on November 5, 1689, to commemorate the first anniversary of William's landing in England.

Psalm LXXV, verses 6, 7.

For Promotion cometh neither from the East, nor
from the West, nor from the South.
But God is the Judge; He putteth down one, and setteth up another. . . .

I⸺T has been proved in all sorts of government, that as the sovereign power in every country or nation is of God, so they that are invested with it, whether one or many, are in the place of God, and have their promotion from him: which was the first part of the doctrine of this text.

The second part is, that the transferring of this power from one to another, is the act of God. And this he does proceeding judicially, as being judge, saith our Psalmist.

Here are two things to be considered. First, that it is God that does this; and secondly, that he does it judicially.

For the first of these, that the transferring of power from one to another is the act of God, this adds much to that which went before in the text. It shows that God

has such an interest in the disposing of power, as none can pretend to but himself.

Men have their part in setting up what they cannot put down again. It is a woman's consent makes a man be her husband, the Fellows of a college choose one to be their head, a corporation choose one to be their mayor: All these do only choose the person, they do not give him the authority. It is the law that gives that, and that law so binds their hands that they cannot undo what they have done.

No more can a nation undo its own act, in choosing men into sovereign power. I do not say but they may choose men into government, expressly with that condition, that they shall be accountable to the people; and then the government remains in the body of the nation, it is that which we properly call a commonwealth. But for sovereign princes and kings, even where they are chosen by the nation; and much more in hereditary kingdoms; as they have their authority from God, so they are only accountable to him. For he is the only potentate, King of Kings, and Lord of Lords. He alone both makes kings by his sovereign power, and by the same

From William Lloyd, *A Discourse of God's Ways of Disposing of Kingdoms* (London, 1691), pp. 17–25, 27–28, 61–67.

he can unmake them when he pleases. . . .

This can be understood of nothing else but the conquest of one prince over another. For what one resigns by a voluntary act, he is said to lay down, or to give it up to another. But putting down is the act of a superior, by which one's place is taken from him against his will. Now God being the superior that does this by the act of his providence, it must be such an act as gives the power from *one* against his will, to *another* whom God is pleased to set up in his stead. Thus in giving one prince a conquest over another, he thereby puts one in possession of the other's dominions, he makes the other's subjects become his subjects, or his slaves, accordingly as they come in upon conditions, or at the will of the conqueror. In short, he giveth him the whole right and power of the other prince. . . .

As a judge, he [God] administreth judgment and justice both which are said to be the habitation of his throne. Particularly, when he decrees a conquest of any king or kingdom; it is either as a *judgment* on them for offenses against himself, or it is by way of *justice* to others whom they have injured. And both these ways he does what is best, for the glory of God, and the good of mankind. . . .

So it commonly happens to those kings that, living in a set[t]led kingdom, will not govern according to the laws thereof. It is a breach of faith, not only to their people, but to God also, where they are sworn to the observing of laws. And though they are not therefore to be deposed by the people, yet they cannot escape the vengeance of God, who ordinarily punishes them with the natural effects of their sin.

Thus in the case of not execution of laws, especially those that are a check upon irreligion and immorality, the very neglect of the due administration of justice, though it seems to be nothing at present, yet in time it will destroy the government. It bringeth the people into a contempt of authority, and they are not much to be blamed for it, for what are they the better for such a government? It lets them loose to all manner of sins, many of which are destructive to society, and all expose them to the wrath of God. Both these ways they are disposed for rebellion at home; and so enfeebled withal, that they cannot withstand a foreign enemy. In this corrupt and weak estate of a government, it is almost impossible that there should not be an alteration.

On the other hand, if a prince will have no law but his will, if he tramples and oppresseth his people, their patience will not hold out always, they will at one time or other show themselves to be but men. At least they will have no heart to fight for their oppressor. So that if a foreign enemy breaks in upon him, he is gone without remedy, unless God interpose. But how can that be, when God is judge himself? Should the judge hinder the doing of justice? It is God's work that foreigner comes to do, howbeit he meaneth not so. He means nothing perhaps, but the satisfying of his own lust. But though he knoweth it not, he is sent in God's message: for which all things being prepared by natural causes, and God not hindering his own work, but rather hastening it, no wonder that it succeeds, and that oftentimes very easily. . . .

In the way of justice, God acts as a judge between two sovereign powers, when they bring their causes before him; that is, when they make war upon one another. And when he seeth his time, that is, when he finds the cause ripe for judgment, if it proceeds so far, then he gives sentence for him that is injured, against him that hath done the injury. The effect of this sentence is a just conquest; and that is the other way in which God, proceeding judicially, puts down one, and sets up another.

That this may be the better understood, there are four things to be considered particularly.

First, That war is an appeal to the justice of God.

Secondly, That none can be parties to this, but they that are in sovereign power.

Thirdly, That to make it a just war, there must be a just and sufficient cause.

Fourthly, That conquest in such a war is a decisive judgment of God, and gives one a right to the dominions that he has conquered from the other.

That war is an appeal to God, this appears in the nature of the thing. For it is the act of two parties that differ about their right. And they put it upon such an issue as none but God can give. For both agree in effect, that the right shall be adjudged to him that has the victory. And it is God alone that is the giver of victory. . . .

Upon this ground it has been commonly judged by the law of nations, that the right goes along with the possession. Of this we see examples in every revolution that happens in this or any other kingdom. When a king is driven out with any colour of right, the neighbouring princes and states make no great difficulty of applying themselves to him that comes in his stead; wherein though perhaps they too much follow their own interest, yet it cannot be said that what they do is against the law of nations. But what should subjects do in this case? Of this we have an example in the people of God, when they passed successively under the yoke of . . . four great monarchs. . . . It is likely that each of those kings that got the power over them, first declared the cause of the war that he made upon their former lords. In that case, though they could not judge of the cause, whether it was just or unjust, yet no doubt they did well in adhering to him that was in present possession. Thus we see they did to Darius, till such time as they found themselves in the power of the enemy: but then, the same reason being turned on his side, they thought it necessary to preserve themselves and their country, by yielding to him, who had a just cause of war for aught they knew, and so far as they could judge by the success, it had God's approbation.

To a people that are in such a case, it is no small comfort, that whatsoever doubt they may have of the cause of the war, yet there is no doubt at all concerning their duty. There is nothing more certain than this, that they ought to preserve themselves, if they can do it lawfully. But it is lawful for them to forbear fighting, when they are unsatisfied of the cause: And if their own prince is not able to protect them, it is lawful for them to take protection elsewhere. Therefore, in case of invasion for a cause which is just for aught they know, it is lawful for them to live quietly under the invader: nay it is not only lawful, but their duty (as hath been already shown) to acquiesce in his government, when he comes to be in possession.

But when they are certain that a war is made upon their prince for just cause; that is, when they plainly see he hath drawn it upon himself, by making it not only lawful, but necessary for another prince to invade him for his own preservation; What are the people to do in this case? No doubt they ought first to have a care of their souls, and not to endanger them by being partakers of other men's sins. They cannot but see, that, by engaging in the war, they abet their own prince in his injustice; though not in his doing the injury, yet in continuing what is done, and in his not giving reparation. And therefore they are subject to the same punishment with him. Nay their condition is worse than his: For he may shift for himself, and leave them and all they have to be a prey to the enemy: Who by right of war may do with them and theirs what he pleases. It is therefore certainly their wisest course to keep themselves free from all offense, both towards God and towards man: That having had no part in the cause of the war, they may not be involved in the ill consequences of it. And this they have reason to expect from a generous enemy, that he will use the right of war against them that desire to live peaceably. Much more, if he hath declared he would not hurt them that should not resist him, they have reason to trust a just prince upon his declaration. And if he went so far as to declare, that upon their submission they should enjoy the benefit of their own laws; then, although it should come to a conquest, they may reasonably expect to be in no worse condition under the stranger, than they were under their own prince: They have his faith engaged to them for this.

But if the stranger declares he makes war in defense of another king's subjects, as (we have shown,) he may lawfully do, when he finds himself in danger of suffering by that king's oppression of his own people; in this case, they are first to consider, whether it is a mere pretense, or whether there be a real ground for his declaration. If they find there is a just and sufficient ground for it, they see in effect, that it is through them that he is struck at; and therefore the war is not so much his, as their own. It is true according to our doctrine, they are united to their prince as a wife to her husband; so that they can no more right themselves by arms, than she can sue her husband while the bond of marriage continues. Yet as, when her husband uses her extremely ill, she may complain of him to the judge, who, if he sees cause, may dissolve the marriage by his sentence; and after that she is at liberty to sue him as well as any other man: So a people may cry to the Lord by reason of their oppression, and he may raise them up a deliverer, that shall take the government into his hands; (a foreign prince may lawfully do this, as hath been already shown;) and then they are not only free to defend themselves, but are obliged to join with him, against their oppressor.

For the people's union with their prince;

though it cannot be dissolved but by a sentence from God; yet by the prince's own act it may be so loosened, that it may be next to dissolution. The laws are the bond of union between prince and people: By these, as the prince holds his prerogative, so do the people their just rights and liberties. Now suppose a people so oppressed by their prince, that their laws being trodden underfoot, they are in danger of losing not only their temporal rights, but, as much as can be, their eternal: In this case, there's no doubt that the oppressor and the oppressed become two parties, being distinguished by the most different interests that can be in the world.

In this case, if another prince, having a just cause of war, is so far concerned for such a people, as to take them into his care, and to declare that he makes the war for their deliverance: The effect of this war, though we may call it a conquest, because it has resemblance of it, yet it cannot be properly so in any respect; whether we consider the prince on whom it is made, or the people that have their deliverance by it.

As to him, it is properly an eviction by the just sentence of God; who thus puts him out of a trust, that he abused to the hurt of them for whose sakes it was given him. And as to the people, it cannot be a conquest over them, who are so far from having the war made against them, that it was made chiefly for their sakes. If there be any pretense of a conquest, it is only over them that were their oppressors. But as for them that were oppressed, it makes altogether on their side; so that they are the conquerors in effect, for they have the benefit of it: And he that obtained this for them hath a much more glorious title than that of a conqueror, for he is properly their restorer and deliverer. . . .

Revolution and the Natural Right of Rebellion

JOHN LOCKE

John Locke, born in 1632, became famous only in the last years of his life. He had been a prominent member of Shaftesbury's household, contributing much to Whig political philosophy. He shared his master's exile after the Oxford Parliament, during which time he preoccupied himself with the nature of political sovereignty. The product of his thinking appeared in print when he returned to England with the Revolution. His vast philosophical contributions affected the fields of government, psychology, religion, education, and economics. He served in a number of posts under William and Mary until his death in 1704.

To understand political power aright, and derive it from its original, we must consider what state all men are naturally in, and that is a state of perfect freedom to order their actions and dispose of their possessions and persons as they think fit, within the bounds of the law of nature, without asking leave, or depending upon the will of any other man.

A state also of equality, wherein all the power and jurisdiction is reciprocal, no one having more than another; there being nothing more evident than that creatures of the same species and rank, promiscuously born to all the same advantages of nature, and the use of the same faculties, should also be equal one amongst another without subordination or subjection, unless the Lord and Master of them all should by any manifest declaration of His will set one above another, and confer on him by an evident and clear appointment an undoubted right to dominion and sovereignty. . . .

But though this be a state of liberty, yet it is not a state of license; though man in

that state have an uncontrollable liberty to dispose of his person or possessions, yet he has not liberty to destroy himself, or so much as any creature in his possession, but where some nobler use than its bare preservation calls for it. The state of nature has a law of nature to govern it, which obliges every one; and reason, which is that law, teaches all mankind who will but consult it, that, being all equal and independent, no one ought to harm another in his life, health, liberty, or possessions. For men being all the workmanship of one omnipotent and infinitely wise Maker— all the servants of one sovereign Master, sent into the world by His order, and about His business—they are His property, whose workmanship they are, made to last during His, not one another's pleasure; and being furnished with like faculties, sharing all in one community of nature, there cannot be supposed any such subordination among us, that may authorize us to destroy one another, as if we were made for one another's uses, as the inferior ranks of creatures are for ours. Every one, as he is bound

From John Locke, *Treatise of Civil Government and a Letter Concerning Toleration*, ed. by Charles L. Sherman (New York, 1937). (Copyright, 1937, D. Appleton-Century Company, Inc.), and reprinted by their permission, pp. 5, 6–7, 18–19, 56–58, 82, 83, 85, 88–89, 143–147, 163–164.

to preserve himself, and not to quit his station willfully, so, by the like reason, when his own preservation comes not in competition, ought he, as much as he can, to preserve the rest of mankind, and not, unless it be to justice on an offender, take away or impair the life, or what tends to the preservation of the life, the liberty, health, limb, or goods of another. . . .

God, who hath given the world to men in common, hath also given them reason to make use of it to the best advantage of life and convenience. The earth and all that is therein is given to men for the support and comfort of their being. And though all the fruits it naturally produces, and beasts it feeds, belong to mankind in common, as they are produced by the spontaneous hand of nature; and nobody has originally a private dominion exclusive of the rest of mankind in any of them as they are thus in their natural state; yet being given for the use of men, there must of necessity be a means to appropriate them some way or other before they can be of any use or at all beneficial to any particular man. The fruit or venison which nourishes the wild Indian, who knows no enclosure, and is still a tenant in common, must be his, and so his, i.e., a part of him, that another can no longer have any right to it, before it can do any good for the support of his life.

Though the earth and all inferior creatures be common to all men, yet every man has a property in his own person; this nobody has any right to but himself. The labour of his body and the work of his hands we may say are properly his. Whatsoever, then, he removes out of the state that nature hath provided and left it in, he hath mixed his labour with, and joined to it something that is his own, and thereby makes it his property. It being by him removed from the common state nature placed it in, it hath by this labour something annexed to it that excludes the common right of other men. For this labour being the unquestionable property of the labourer, no man but he can have a right to what that is once joined to, at least where there is enough, and as good left in common for others. . . .

Man being born, as has been proved, with a title to perfect freedom, and an uncontrolled enjoyment of all the rights and privileges of the law of nature equally with any other man or number of men in the world, hath by nature a power not only to preserve his property—that is, his life, liberty, and estate—against the injuries and attempts of other men, but to judge of and punish the breaches of that law in others as he is persuaded the offense deserves, even with death itself, in crimes where the heinousness of the fact in his opinion requires it. But because no political society can be nor subsist without having in itself the power to preserve the property, and, in order thereunto, punish the offenses of all those of that society, there, and there only, is political society, where every one of the members hath quitted this natural power, resigned it up into the hands of the community in all cases that exclude him not from appealing for protection to the law established by it; and thus all private judgment of every particular member being excluded, the community comes to be umpire; and by understanding indifferent rules and men authorized by the community for their execution, decides all the differences that may happen between any members of that society concerning any matter of right, and punishes those offenses which any member hath committed against the society with such penalties as the law has established; whereby it is easy to discern who are and who are not in political society together. Those who are united into one body, and have a common established law and judicature to appeal to, with authority to decide controversies between them and punish offenders, are in civil society one with another; but those who have no such common appeal—I mean on earth—are still in the state of nature, each being, where there is no other, judge for himself and executioner, which is, as I have before shown it, the perfect state of nature.

And thus the commonwealth comes by a power to set down what punishment shall belong to the several transgressions which they think worthy of it committed amongst the members of that society, which is the power of making laws, as well as it has the power to punish any injury done unto any of its members by anyone that is not of it, which is the power of war and peace; and all this for the preservation of the property of all the members of that society as far as is possible. But though every man entered into civil society, has quitted his power to punish offenses against the law of nature in prosecution of his own private judgment, yet with the judgment of offenses, which he has given up to the legislative in all cases where he can appeal to the magistrate, he has given a right to the commonwealth to employ his force for the execution of the judgments of the commonwealth whenever he shall be called to it; which, indeed, are his own judgments, they being made by himself or his representative. And herein we have the original of the legislative and executive power of civil society, which is to judge by standing laws how far offenses are to be punished when committed within the commonwealth, and also by occasional judgments founded on the present circumstances of the fact, how far injuries from without are to be vindicated; and in both these to employ all the force of all the members when there shall be need.

Wherever, therefore, any number of men so unite into one society, as to quit every one his executive power of the law of nature, and to resign it to the public, there, and there only, is a political, or civil society. And this is done wherever any number of men, in the state of nature, enter into society to make one people one body politic, under one supreme government, or else when anyone joins himself to, and incorporates with, any government already made. For hereby he authorizes the society, or, which is all one, the legislative thereof, to make laws for him, as the public good of the society shall require, to the execution whereof his own assistance (as to his own decrees) is due. And this puts men out of a state of nature into that of a commonwealth, by setting up a judge on earth with authority to determine all the controversies and redress the injuries that may happen to any member of the commonwealth; which judge is the legislative, or magistrates appointed by it. And wherever there are any number of men, however associated, that have no such decisive power to appeal to, there they are still in the state of nature. . . .

If man in the state of nature be so free, as has been said, if he be absolute lord of his own person and possessions, equal to the greatest, and subject to nobody, why will he part with his freedom, this empire, and subject himself to the dominion and control of any other power? To which, it is obvious to answer, that though in the state of nature he hath such a right, yet the enjoyment of it is very uncertain, and constantly exposed to the invasions of others. For all being kings as much as he, every man his equal, and the greater part no strict observers of equity and justice, the enjoyment of the property he has in this state is very unsafe, very unsecure. This makes him willing to quit this condition, which, however free, is full of fears and continual dangers; and it is not without reason that he seeks out and is willing to join in society with others, who are already united, or have a mind to unite, for the mutual preservation of their lives, liberties, and estates, which I call by the general name, property.

The great and chief end, therefore, of men's uniting into commonwealths, and putting themselves under government, is the preservation of their property; to which in the state of nature there are many things wanting. . . .

Thus mankind, notwithstanding all the

privileges of the state of nature, being but in an ill condition, while they remain in it, are quickly driven into society. Hence it comes to pass that we seldom find any number of men live any time together in this state. The inconveniences that they are therein exposed to by the irregular and uncertain exercise of the power every man has of punishing the transgressions of others, make them take sanctuary under the established laws of government, and therein seek the preservation of their property. It is this makes them so willingly give up every one his single power of punishing, to be exercised by such alone, as shall be appointed to it amongst them; and by such rules as the community, or those authorized by them to that purpose, shall agree on. And in this we have the original right and rise of both the legislative and executive power, as well as of the governments and societies themselves. . . .

But though men when they enter into society give up the equality, liberty and executive power they had in the state of nature into the hands of the society, to be so far disposed of by the legislative as the good of the society shall require; yet it being only with an intention in every one the better to preserve himself, his liberty and property (for no rational creature can be supposed to change his condition with an intention to be worse), the power of the society, or legislative constituted by them, can never be supposed to extend farther than the common good, but is obliged to secure every one's property by providing against those . . . defects above-mentioned that made the state of nature so unsafe and uneasy. And so whoever has the legislative or supreme power of any commonwealth is bound to govern by established standing laws, promulgated and known to the people, and not by extemporary decrees; by indifferent and upright judges, who are to decide controversies by those laws; and to employ the force of the community at home only in the execution of such laws, or abroad, to prevent or redress foreign injuries, and secure the community from inroads and invasion. And all this to be directed to no other end but the peace, safety, and public good of the people. . . .

The great end of men's entering into society being the enjoyment of their properties in peace and safety, and the great instrument and means of that being the laws established in that society: the first and fundamental positive law of all commonwealths, is the establishing of the legislative power; as the first and fundamental natural law, which is to govern even the legislative itself, is the preservation of the society, and (as far as will consist with the public good) of every person in it. This legislative is not only the supreme power of the commonwealth, but sacred and unalterable in the hands where the community have once placed it; nor can any edict of anybody else, in what form soever conceived, or by what power soever backed, have the force and obligation of a law, which has not its sanction from that legislative which the public has chosen and appointed. For without this the law could not have that, which is absolutely necessary to its being a law, the consent of the society over whom nobody can have a power to make laws; but by their own consent, and by authority received from them; and therefore all the obedience, which by the most solemn ties anyone can be obliged to pay, ultimately terminates in this supreme power, and is directed by those laws which it enacts; nor can any oaths to any foreign power whatsoever, or any domestic subordinate power discharge any member of the society from his obedience to the legislative, acting pursuant to their trust; nor oblige him to any obedience contrary to the laws so enacted, or farther than they do allow; it being ridiculous to imagine one can be tied ultimately to obey any power in the society which is not the supreme. . . .

. . . Civil society being a state of peace amongst those who are of it, from whom the state of war is excluded by the umpirage which they have provided in their legislative for the ending all differences that may arise amongst any of them, it is in their legislative that the members of a commonwealth are united and combined together in one coherent living body. This is the soul that gives form, life, and unity to the commonwealth. From hence the several members have their mutual influence, sympathy, and connection. And, therefore, when the legislative is broken or dissolved, dissolution and death follow. For the essence and union of the society consisting in having one will, the legislative, when once established by the majority, has the declaring and, as it were, keeping of, that will. The constitution of the legislative is the first and fundamental act of the society, whereby provision is made for the continuation of their union, under the direction of persons and bonds of laws made by persons authorized thereunto by the consent and appointment of the people, without which no one man or number of men amongst them can have authority of making laws that shall be binding to the rest. When any one or more shall take upon them to make laws, whom the people have not appointed so to do, they make laws without authority, which the people are not therefore bound to obey; by which means they come again to be out of subjection, and may constitute to themselves a new legislative, as they think best, being in full liberty to resist the force of those who without authority would impose anything upon them. Everyone is at the disposure of his own will when those who had by the delegation of the society the declaring of the public will, are excluded from it, and others usurp the place who have no such authority or delegation.

This being usually brought about by such in the commonwealth who misuse the power they have, it is hard to consider it aright, and know at whose door to lay it, without knowing the form of government in which it happens. Let us suppose, then, the legislative placed in the concurrence of three distinct persons.

1. A single hereditary person having the constant supreme executive power, and with it the power of convoking and dissolving the other two within certain periods of time.

2. An assembly of hereditary nobility.

3. An assembly of representatives chosen *pro tempore* by the people. Such a form of government supposed, it is evident,

First, That when such a single person or prince sets up his own arbitrary will in place of the laws which are the will of the society, declared by the legislative, then the legislative is changed. For that being in effect the legislative whose rules and laws are put in execution and required to be obeyed when other laws are set up, and other rules pretended and enforced, than what the legislative constituted by the society have enacted, it is plain that the legislative is changed. Whoever introduces new laws, not being thereunto authorized by the fundamental appointment of the society, or subverts the old, disowns and overturns the power by which they were made, and so sets up a new legislative.

Secondly, When the prince hinders the legislative from assembling in its due time, or from acting freely, pursuant to those ends for which it was constituted, the legislative is altered. For it is not a certain number of men, no, nor their meeting, unless they have also freedom of debating and leisure of perfecting what is for the good of the society, wherein the legislative consists. When these are taken away or altered so as to deprive the society of the due exercise of their power, the legislative is truly altered. For it is not names that constitute governments, but the use and exercise of those powers that were intended to accompany them; so that he who takes away the freedom, or hinders the acting of the legislative in its due seasons, in effect takes away the legislative, and puts an end to the government.

Thirdly, When, by the arbitrary power of the prince, the electors or ways of elections are altered, without the consent and contrary to the common interest of the people, there also the legislative is altered.

For if others than those whom the society hath authorized thereunto, do choose, or in another way than what the society hath prescribed, those chosen are not the legislative appointed by the people.

Fourthly, The delivery also of the people into the subjection of foreign power, either by the prince, or by the legislative, is certainly a change of the legislative, and so a dissolution of the government. For the end why people entered into society being to be preserved one entire, free, independent society, to be governed by its own laws, this is lost whenever they are given up into the power of another.

Why in such a constitution as this the dissolution of the government in these cases is to be imputed to the prince, is evident; because he, having the force, treasure, and offices of the state to employ, and often persuading himself, or being flattered by others, that, as supreme magistrate he is incapable of control, he alone is in a condition to make great advances towards such changes, under pretense of lawful authority, and has it in his hands to terrify or suppress opposers, as factious, seditious, and enemies to the government. Whereas no other part of the legislative or people is capable by themselves to attempt any alteration of the legislative, without open and visible rebellion, apt enough to be taken notice of, which, when it prevails, produces effects very little different from foreign conquest. Besides, the prince in such a form of government, having the power of dissolving the other parts of the legislative, and thereby rendering them private persons, they can never, in opposition to him, or without his concurrence, alter the legislative by a law, his consent being necessary to give any of their decrees that sanction. But yet so far as the other parts of the legislative any way contribute to any attempt upon the government, and do either promote, or not, what lies in them, hinder such designs, they are guilty, and partake in this, which is certainly the greatest crime men can be guilty of one towards another.

There is one way more whereby such a government may be dissolved, and that is, when he who has the supreme executive power neglects and abandons that charge, so that the laws already made can no longer be put in execution. This is demonstratively to reduce all to anarchy, and so effectually to dissolve the government. For laws not being made for themselves, but to be by their execution the bonds of the society, to keep every part of the body politic, in its due place and function, when that totally ceases, the government visibly ceases, and the people become a confused multitude without order or connection. Where there is no longer the administration of justice, for the securing of men's rights, nor any remaining power within the community to direct the force, or provide for the necessities of the public, there certainly is no government left. Where the laws cannot be executed, it is all one as if there were no laws; and a government without laws is, I suppose, a mystery in politics, inconceivable to human capacity, and inconsistent with human society.

In these and the like cases, when the government is dissolved, the people are at liberty to provide for themselves by erecting a new legislative, differing from the other, by the change of persons, or form, or both, as they shall find it most for their safety and good. For the society can never, by the fault of another, lose the native and original right it has to preserve itself, which can only be done by a settled legislative, and a fair and impartial execution of the laws made by it. But the state of mankind is not so miserable that they are not capable of using this remedy, till it be too late to look for any. To tell people they may provide for themselves by erecting a new legislative, when by oppression, artifice, or being delivered over to a foreign power, their old one is gone, is only to tell them they may expect relief when it is too late, and the evil is past cure. This is in effect no more than to bid them first be slaves, and then to take care of their liberty; and when their chains are on tell them they may act like free men. This, if barely so, is rather mockery than relief; and men can never be secure from tyranny if there be no means to escape it till they are perfectly under it. And therefore it is that they have not only a right to get out of it, but to prevent it. . . .

If a controversy arise betwixt a prince and some of the people in a matter where the law is silent or doubtful, and the thing be of great consequence, I should think the proper umpire in such a case should be the body of the people; for in cases where the prince hath a trust reposed in him, and is dispensed from the common ordinary rules of the law; there, if any men find themselves aggrieved, and think the prince acts contrary to or beyond that trust, who so proper to judge as the body of the people (who at first lodged that trust in him) how far they meant it should extend? But if the prince or whoever they be in the administration decline that way of determination, the appeal then lies nowhere but to heaven; force between either persons who have no known superior on earth, or which permits no appeal to a judge on earth, being properly a state of war, wherein the appeal lies only to heaven, and in that state the injured party must judge for himself when he will think fit to make use of that appeal and put himself upon it.

To conclude, the power that every individual gave the society when he entered into it, can never revert to the individuals again as long as the society lasts, but will always remain in the community, because without this there can be no community, no commonwealth, which is contrary to the original agreement; so also when the society hath placed the legislative in any assembly of men to continue in them and their successors, with direction and authority for providing such successors, the legislative can never revert to the people whilst that government lasts, because having provided a legislative with power to continue forever, they have given up their political power to the legislative and cannot resume it. But if they have set limits to the duration of their legislative, and made this supreme power in any person or assembly only temporary; or else when by the miscarriages of those in authority it is forfeited; upon the forfeiture, or at the determination of the time set, it reverts to the society, and the people have a right to act as supreme, and continue the legislative in themselves; or place it in a new form, or new hands as they think good. . . .

PART II: THE TRIUMPH OF WHIG THEORY IN MODERN INTERPRETATION

The Revolution in the Age of Liberal Reform

THOMAS BABINGTON MACAULAY

Macaulay was born in 1800 and his life span includes the years of England's pre-eminence in commerce and political influence. He entered politics as a crusader against slavery and political restriction of Jews and Catholics. He participated in the debates for the Great Reform Bill of 1832, which to him marked the high point of English institutional development. Later, he became noted for his reforms in Indian education, as a literary critic, and as a historian of the late seventeenth century. His great *History of England*, from which the following is taken, is in part an attempt to explain why England became so great, and why she remained stable while continental countries passed from crisis to crisis (the first volume appeared during the Revolutions of 1848). He died with the task incompleted in 1859.

I PURPOSE to write the history of England from the accession of King James the Second down to a time which is within the memory of men still living. I shall recount the errors which, in a few months, alienated a loyal gentry and priesthood from the House of Stuart. I shall trace the course of that revolution which terminated the long struggle between our sovereigns and their parliaments, and bound up together the rights of the people and the title of the reigning dynasty. I shall relate how the new settlement was, during many troubled years, successfully defended against foreign and domestic enemies; how, under that settlement, the authority of law and the security of property were found to be compatible with a liberty of discussion and of individual action never before known; how, from the auspicious union of order and freedom, sprang a prosperity of which the annals of human affairs had furnished no example; how our country, from a state of ignominious vassalage, rapidly rose to the place of umpire among European powers; how her opulence and her martial glory grew together; how, by wise and resolute good faith, was gradually established a public credit fruitful of marvels which to the statesmen of any former age would have seemed incredible; how a gigantic commerce gave birth to a maritime power, compared with which every other maritime power, ancient or modern, sinks into insignificance; how Scotland, after ages of enmity, was at length united to England, not merely by legal bonds, but by indissoluble ties of interest and affection; how, in America, the British colonies rapidly became far mightier and wealthier

From *The History of England from the Accession of James II* by Thomas Babington Macaulay. Everyman's Library. Reprinted by permission of E. P. Dutton & Co., Inc., vol. I, pp. 1–3, 210; vol. II, pp. 350–351, 374–381.

than the realms which Cortes and Pizarro had added to the dominion of Charles the Fifth; how, in Asia, British adventurers founded an empire not less splendid and more durable than that of Alexander. . . .

. . . Unless I greatly deceive myself, the general effect of this chequered narrative will be to excite thankfulness in all religious minds, and hope in the breasts of all patriots. For the history of our country during the last hundred and sixty years is eminently the history of physical, of moral, and of intellectual improvement. Those who compare the age on which their lot has fallen with a golden age which exists only in their imagination may talk of degeneracy and decay: but no man who is correctly informed as to the past will be disposed to take a morose or desponding view of the present. . . .

. . . While every part of the Continent, from Moscow to Lisbon, has been the theatre of bloody and devastating wars, no hostile standard has been seen here but as a trophy. While revolutions have taken place all around us, our government has never once been subverted by violence. During a hundred years there has been in our island no tumult of sufficient importance to be called an insurrection. The law has never been borne down either by popular fury or by regal tyranny. Public credit has been held sacred. The administration of justice has been pure. Even in times which might by Englishmen be justly called evil times, we have enjoyed what almost every other nation in the world would have considered as an ample measure of civil and religious freedom. Every man has felt entire confidence that the state would protect him in the possession of what had been earned by his diligence and hoarded by his self-denial. Under the benignant influence of peace and liberty, science has flourished, and has been applied to practical purposes on a scale never before known. The consequence is that a change to which the history of the old world furnishes no parallel has taken place in our country. . . .

*   *   *

. . . It was moved [in the House of Commons] that King James the Second, having endeavoured to subvert the constitution of the kingdom by breaking the original contract between King and people, and, by the advice of Jesuits and other wicked persons, having violated the fundamental laws, and having withdrawn himself out of the kingdom, had abdicated the government, and that the throne had thereby become vacant.

This resolution has been many times subjected to criticism as minute and severe as was ever applied to any sentence written by man: and perhaps there never was a sentence written by man which would bear such criticism less. That a King by grossly abusing his power may forfeit it is true. That a King, who absconds without making any provision for the administration, and leaves his people in a state of anarchy, may, without any violent straining of language, be said to have abdicated his functions is also true. But no accurate writer would affirm that long continued misgovernment and desertion, added together, make up an act of abdication. It is evident too that the mention of the Jesuits and other evil advisers of James weakens, instead of strengthening, the case against him. For surely more indulgence is due to a man misled by pernicious counsel than to a man who goes wrong from the mere impulse of his own mind. It is idle, however, to examine these memorable words as we should examine a chapter of Aristotle or of Hobbes. Such words are to be considered, not as words, but as deeds. If they effect that which they are intended to effect, they are rational, though they may be contradictory. If they fail of attaining their end, they are absurd, though they carry demonstration with them. Logic admits of no compromise. The essence of politics is compromise. It is therefore not strange that some of the most important and most useful political instruments in the world should be among the most illogical compositions that ever were penned. The object of Somers, of Maynard, and of the other eminent men who shaped this celebrated motion was, not to leave to posterity a model of definition and partition, but to make the restoration of a tyrant impossible, and to place on the throne a sovereign under whom law and liberty might be secure. This object they attained by using language which, in a philosophical treatise, would justly be reprehended as inexact and confused. They cared little whether their major agreed with their conclusion, if the major secured two hundred votes, and the conclusion two hundred more. In fact the one beauty of the resolution is its inconsistency. There was a phrase for every subdivision of the majority. The mention of the original contract gratified the disciples of Sidney. The word abdication conciliated politicians of a more timid school. There were doubtless many fervent Protestants who were pleased with the censure cast on the Jesuits. To the real statesman the single important clause was that which declared the throne vacant; and, if that clause could be carried, he cared little by what preamble it might be introduced. . . .

Thus was consummated the English Revolution. When we compare it with those revolutions which have, during the last sixty years, overthrown so many ancient governments, we cannot but be struck by its peculiar character. Why that character was so peculiar is sufficiently obvious, and yet seems not to have been always understood either by eulogists or by censors.

The continental revolutions of the eighteenth and nineteenth centuries took place in countries where all trace of the limited monarchy of the middle ages had long been effaced. The right of the prince to make laws and to levy money had, during many generations, been undisputed. His throne was guarded by a great regular army. His administration could not, without extreme peril, be blamed even in the mildest terms. His subjects held their personal liberty by no other tenure than his pleasure. Not a single institution was left which had, within the memory of the oldest man, afforded efficient protection to the subject against the utmost excess of tyranny. Those great councils which had once curbed the regal power had sunk into oblivion. Their composition and their privileges were known only to antiquaries. We cannot wonder, therefore, that, when men who had been thus ruled succeeded in wresting supreme power from a government which they had long in secret hated, they should have been impatient to demolish and unable to construct, that they should have been fascinated by every specious novelty, that they should have proscribed every title, ceremony, and phrase associated with the old system, and that, burning away with disgust from their own national precedents and traditions, they should have sought for principles of government in the writings of theorists, or aped, with ignorant and ungraceful affectation, the patriots of Athens and Rome. As little can we wonder that the violent action of the revolution spirit should have been followed by reaction equally violent, and that confusion should speedily have engendered despotism sterner than that from which it had sprung.

Had we been in the same situation; had Strafford succeeded in his favourite scheme of Thorough; had he formed an army as numerous and as well disciplined as that which, a few years later, was formed by Cromwell; had a series of judicial decisions, similar to that which was pronounced by the Exchequer Chamber in the case of ship-money, transferred to the crown the right of taxing the people; had the Star Chamber and the High Commission continued to fine, mutilate, and imprison every man who dared to raise his voice against the government; had the press been as completely enslaved here as at Vienna or at Naples; had our Kings gradually drawn to themselves the whole legislative power; had six generations of Englishmen passed away without a single session of Parliament; and had we then at length risen up in some moment of wild excitement against our masters, what an outbreak would that have been! With what a crash, heard and felt to the farthest ends of the world, would the whole vast fabric of society have fallen! How many thousands of exiles, once the most prosperous and the most refined members of this great community, would have begged their bread in continental cities, or have sheltered their heads under huts of bark in the uncleared forests of America! How often should we have seen the pavement of London piled up in barricades, the houses dinted with bullets, the gutters foaming with blood! How many times should we have rushed wildly from extreme to extreme, sought refuge from anarchy in despotism, and been again driven by despotism into anarchy! How many years of blood and confusion would it have cost us to learn the very rudiments of political science! How many childish theories would have duped us! How many rude and ill poised constitutions should we have set up, only to see them tumble down! Happy would it have been for us if a sharp discipline of half a century had sufficed to educate us into a capacity of enjoying true freedom.

These calamities our Revolution averted. It was a revolution strictly defensive, and had prescription and legitimacy on its side. Here, and here only, a limited monarchy of the thirteenth century had come down unimpaired to the seventeenth century. Our parliamentary institutions were in full vigour. The main principles of our government were excellent. They were not, indeed, formally and exactly set forth in a single written instrument; but they were to be found scattered over our ancient and noble statutes; and, what was of far greater moment, they had been engraven on the hearts of Englishmen during four hundred years. That, without the consent of the representatives of the nation, no legislative act could be passed, no tax imposed, no regular soldiery kept up, that no man could be imprisoned, even for a day, by the arbitrary will of the sovereign, that no tool of power could plead the royal command as

a justification for violating any right of the humblest subject, were held, both by Whigs and Tories, to be fundamental laws of the realm. A realm of which these were the fundamental laws stood in no need of a new constitution.

But, though a new constitution was not needed, it was plain that changes were required. The misgovernment of the Stuarts, and the troubles which that misgovernment had produced, sufficiently proved that there was somewhere a defect in our polity; and that defect it was the duty of the Convention to discover and to supply.

Some questions of great moment were still open to dispute. Our constitution had begun to exist in times when statesmen were not much accustomed to frame exact definitions. Anomalies, therefore, inconsistent with its principles and dangerous to its very existence, had sprung up almost imperceptibly, and, not having, during many years, caused any serious inconvenience, had gradually acquired the force of prescription. The remedy for these evils was to assert the rights of the people in such language as should terminate all controversy, and to declare that no precedent could justify any violation of those rights.

When this had been done it would be impossible for our rulers to misunderstand the law: but, unless something more were done, it was by no means improbable that they might violate it. Unhappily the Church had long taught the nation that hereditary monarchy, alone among our institutions, was divine and inviolable; that the right of the House of Commons to a share in the legislative power was a right merely human, but that the right of the King to the obedience of his people was from above; that the Great Charter was a statute which might be repealed by those who had made it, but that the rule which called the princes of the blood royal to the throne in order of succession was of celestial origin, and that any Act of Parliament inconsistent with that rule was a nullity. It is evident that, in a society in which such superstitions prevail, constitutional freedom must ever be insecure. A power which is regarded merely as the ordinance of man cannot be an efficient check on a power which is regarded as the ordinance of God. It is vain to hope that laws, however excellent, will permanently restrain a King who, in his own opinion, and in that of a great part of his people, has an authority infinitely higher in kind than the authority which belongs to those laws. To deprive royalty of these mysterious attributes, and to establish the principle that Kings reigned by a right in no respect differing from the right by which freeholders chose knights of the shire, or from the right by which Judges granted writs of Habeas Corpus, was absolutely necessary to the security of our liberties.

Thus the Convention had two great duties to perform. The first was to clear the fundamental laws of the realm from ambiguity. The second was to eradicate from the minds, both of the governors and of the governed, the false and pernicious notion that the royal prerogative was something more sublime and holy than those fundamental laws. The former object was attained by the solemn recital and claim with which the Declaration of Right commences; the latter by the resolution which pronounced the throne vacant, and invited William and Mary to fill it.

The change seems small. Not a single flower of the crown was touched. Not a single new right was given to the people. The whole English law, substantive and adjective, was, in the judgment of all the greatest lawyers, of Holt and Treby, of Maynard and Somers, exactly the same after the Revolution as before it. Some controverted points had been decided according to the sense of the best jurists; and there had been a slight deviation from the ordinary course of succession. This was all; and this was enough. . . .

. . . To us, who have lived in the year 1848, it may seem almost an abuse of terms to call a proceeding, conducted with so much deliberation, with so much sobriety, and with such minute attention to prescriptive etiquette, by the terrible name of Revolution.

And yet this revolution, of all revolutions the least violent, has been of all revolutions the most beneficent. It finally decided the great question whether the popular element which had, ever since the age of Fitzwalter and De Montfort, been found in the English polity, should be destroyed by the monarchical element, or should be suffered to develop itself freely, and to become dominant. The strife between the two principles had been long, fierce, and doubtful. It had lasted through four reigns. It had produced seditions, impeachments, rebellions, battles, sieges, proscriptions, judicial massacres. Sometimes liberty, sometimes royalty, had seemed to be on the point of perishing. During many years one half of the energy of England had been employed in counteracting the other half. The executive power and the legislative power had so effectually impeded each other that the state had been of no account in Europe. The King at Arms, who proclaimed William and Mary before Whitehall Gate, did in truth announce that this great struggle was over; that there was entire union between the throne and the Parliament; that England, long dependent and degraded, was again a power of the first rank; that the ancient laws by which the prerogative was bounded would henceforth be held as sacred as the prerogative itself, and would be followed out to all their consequences; that the executive administration would be conducted in conformity with the sense of the representatives of the nation; and that no reform, which the two Houses should, after mature deliberation, propose, would be obstinately withstood by the sovereign. The Declaration of Right, though it made nothing law which had not been law before, contained the germ of the law which gave religious freedom to the Dissenter, of the law which secured the independence of the Judges, of the law which limited the duration of Parliaments, of the law which placed the liberty of the press under the protection of juries, of the law which prohibited the slave trade, of the law which abolished the sacramental test, of the law which relieved the Roman Catholics from civil disabilities, of the law which reformed the representative system, of every good law which has been passed during a hundred and sixty years, of every good law which may hereafter, in the course of ages, be found necessary to promote the public weal, and to satisfy the demands of public opinion.

The highest eulogy which can be pronounced on the revolution of 1688 is this, that it was our last revolution. Several generations have now passed away since any wise and patriotic Englishman has meditated resistance to the established government. In all honest and reflecting minds there is a conviction, daily strengthened by experience, that the means of effecting every improvement which the constitution requires may be found within the constitution itself.

Now, if ever, we ought to be able to appreciate the whole importance of the stand which was made by our forefathers against the House of Stuart. All around us the world is convulsed by the agonies of great nations. Governments which lately seemed likely to stand during ages have been on a sudden shaken and overthrown. The proudest capitals of Western Europe have streamed with civil blood. All evil passions, the thirst of gain and the thirst of vengeance, the antipathy of class to class, the antipathy of race to race, have broken loose from the control of divine and human laws. Fear and anxiety have clouded the faces and depressed the hearts of millions. Trade has been suspended, and industry paralysed. The rich have become poor; and the poor have become poorer. Doctrines hostile to all sciences, to all arts, to all industry, to all domestic charities, doctrines which, if carried into effect, would, in thirty years, undo all that thirty centuries have done for mankind, and would make the fairest provinces of France and Germany as savage as Congo or Patagonia, have been avowed from the tribune and defended by the sword. Europe has been threatened with subjugation by barbarians, compared with whom the barbarians who marched under Attila and Alboin were enlightened and humane. The truest friends of the people have with deep sorrow owned that interests more precious than any political privileges were in jeopardy, and that it might be necessary to sacrifice even liberty in order to save civilisation. Meanwhile in our island the regular course of government has never been for a day interrupted. The few bad men who longed for license and plunder have not had the courage to confront for one moment the strength of a loyal nation, rallied in firm array round a parental throne. And, if it be asked what has made us to differ from others, the answer is that we never lost what others are wildly and blindly seeking to regain. It is because we had a preserving revolution in the seventeenth century that we have not had a destroying revolution in the nineteenth. It is because we had freedom in the midst of servitude that we have order in the midst of anarchy. For the authority of law, for the security of property, for the peace of our streets, for the happiness of our homes, our gratitude is due, under Him who raises and pulls down nations at his pleasure, to the Long Parliament, to the Convention, and to William of Orange. . . .

The Revolution as a Movement
for Democratic Unification

GEORGE MACAULAY TREVELYAN

George Macaulay Trevelyan, born in 1876, is one of the greatest of
Britain's modern historians. Before his retirement in 1951, he was Regius
Professor of Modern History at Cambridge (1927), and later Master of Trinity
College (1940). He is noted for his respect for the Whig tradition, his belief
that scholarship and literary excellence should be united, and his interest in
social history. He died in 1962 at the age of eighty-eight.

WHY do historians regard the Revolution of 1688 as important? And did it deserve the title of "glorious" which was long its distinctive epithet? "The Sensible Revolution" would perhaps have been a more appropriate title and certainly would have distinguished it more clearly as among other revolutions.

But insofar as it was indeed "glorious," in what does its "glory" consist? It is not the Napoleonic brand of glory. It is not to be sought in the glamour of its events, the drama of its scenes, and the heroism of its actors, though these also rouse the imagination and stir the blood. The Seven Bishops passing to the Tower through the kneeling throngs; William's fleet floating into Torbay before the Protestant wind; the flight of James II, following his wife and infant son to France, none of them ever to return—doubtless these are romantic scenes, that live in memory. Such also are the events that followed more bloodily in Scotland and in Ireland—the roaring pass of Killiecrankie, the haggard watch on Londonderry walls, and Boyne water bristling with musket and pike. Yet all these are not, like the fall of the Bastille or Napoleon's Empire, a new birth of time, a new shape of terror. They are spirited variations on themes invented forty years before by a more heroic, creative and imprudent generation.

The Seven Bishops whom James II prosecuted were milder and more conservative men than the Five Members whom Charles I attempted to arrest, yet the second story reads much like a repetition of the first: in both cases the King rashly attacks popular leaders who are protected by the law, and by the mass opinion of the capital. In both cases the King's downfall shortly follows. Much else indeed is very different: there is no English Civil War on the second occasion, for in 1688 even the Cavaliers (renamed Tories) were against the King. But the men of the Revolution, James and William, Danby, Halifax, Sancroft, Dundee, are manipulating forces, parties and ideas which had first been evoked in the days of Laud, Strafford, Pym, Hampden, Hyde, Cromwell, Rupert, Milton and Montrose. In the later Revolution there are no new ideas, for even Toleration had been eagerly discussed round Cromwell's camp-fires. But in 1688

From G. M. Trevelyan, *The English Revolution, 1688–1689* (Oxford, 1938). Reprinted by permission of the Oxford University Press, pp. 7–19, 134, 138–141, 145, 146, 149, 150, 164–166, 245.

there is a very different grouping of the old parties, and a new and happier turn is given to the old issues, in England though not in Ireland, by compromise, agreement and toleration. An heroic age raises questions, but it takes a sensible age to solve them. Roundheads and Cavaliers, high in hope, had broken up the soil, but the Whigs and Tories soberly garnered the harvest.

A certain amount of disillusionment helps to make men wise, and by 1688 men had been doubly disillusioned, first by the rule of the Saints under Cromwell, and then by the rule of the Lord's Anointed under James. Above all, taught by experience, men shrank from another civil war. The burned child fears the fire. The merit of this Revolution lay not in the shouting and the tumult, but in the still, small voice of prudence and wisdom that prevailed through all the din.

The true "glory" of the Revolution lies not in the minimum of violence which was necessary for its success, but in the way of escape from violence which the Revolution Settlement found for future generations of Englishmen. There is nothing specially glorious in the victory which our ancestors managed to win, with the aid of foreign arms, over an ill-advised king who forced an issue with nine-tenths of his English subjects on the fundamentals of law, politics and religion. To have been beaten at such odds would have been national ignominy indeed. The "glory" of that brief and bloodless campaign lies with William, who laid deep and complicated plans and took great risks in coming over at all, rather than with the English who had only to throw up their caps for him with sufficient unanimity when once he and his troops had landed. But it is England's true glory that the cataclysm of James's overthrow was not accompanied by the shedding of English blood either on the field or on the scaffold. The political instincts of our people appeared in the avoidance of a second Civil War, for which all the elements were present. Our enemy Louis XIV of France

had confidently expected that another long period of confusion and strife would ensue in our factious island if William should land there; if he had thought otherwise, he could have threatened the frontiers of Holland, and so prevented his rival from setting sail at all.

But the Convention Parliament of February 1689, by uniting England, baffled the policy of France. By wise compromise it stanched forever the blood feud of Roundhead and Cavalier, of Anglican and Puritan, which had broken out first at Edgehill and Naseby, and bled afresh only four years back at Sedgemoor. Whig and Tory, having risen together in rebellion against James, seized the fleeting moment of their union to fix a new-old form of Government, known in history as the Revolution Settlement. Under it, England has lived at peace within herself ever since. The Revolution Settlement in Church and State proved to have the quality of permanence. It stood almost unaltered until the era of the Reform Bill of 1832. And throughout the successive stages of rapid change that have followed, its fundamentals have remained to bear the weight of the vast democratic superstructure which the nineteenth and twentieth centuries have raised upon its sure foundation. Here, seen at long range, is "glory," burning steadily for 250 years: it is not the fierce, short, destructive blaze of *la gloire*.

The expulsion of James was a revolutionary act, but otherwise the spirit of this strange Revolution was the opposite of revolutionary. It came not to overthrow the law but to confirm it against a law-breaking king. It came not to coerce people into one pattern of opinion in politics or religion, but to give them freedom under and by the law. It was at once liberal and conservative; most revolutions are neither one nor the other, but overthrow the laws, and then tolerate no way of thinking save one. But in our Revolution the two great parties in Church and State united to save the laws of the land from destruction by James; having done so, and having thereby become jointly and severally masters of the situation in February 1689, neither the Whig nor the Tory party would suffer its clients to be any longer subject to persecution, either by the Royal power or by the opposite party in the State. Under these circumstances the keynote of the Revolution Settlement was personal freedom under the law, both in religion and in politics. The most conservative of all revolutions in history was also the most liberal. If James had been overthrown either by the Whigs alone or by the Tories alone, the settlement that followed his downfall would not have been so liberal, or so permanent.

In the realm of thought and religion, individual liberty was secured by the abandonment of the cherished idea that all subjects of the State must also be members of the State Church. The Toleration Act of 1689 granted the right of religious worship, though not complete political equality, to Protestant Dissenters; and so strong was the latitudinarian and tolerant spirit of the age ushered in by the Revolution, that these privileges were soon extended in practice though not in law to the Roman Catholics, against whom the Revolution had in one aspect been specially directed.

The political freedom of the individual was secured in a like spirit, by the abolition of the Censorship (1695), by the milder and less partial administration of political justice, and by the balance of power between the Whig and Tory parties, under whose rival banners almost everyone in some sort found shelter. In these ways the distinctively English idea of the freedom of opinion and the rights of the individual were immensely enhanced by the peculiar character of this Revolution.

James had tried to put the King above Parliament and above the Law. The Revolution, while leaving the King the source of executive authority, subjected him to the Law, which was henceforth to be interpreted by independent and irremovable Judges, and could only be altered by Act of Parliament. At the same time, by the annual Mutiny Act that made the army dependent of Parliament, and by the refusal to grant to William for life the supplies that had been granted for the lives of Charles and James II, the House of Commons obtained a power of bargaining with Government that rendered it even more important than the House of Lords; indeed, from the Revolution onwards the Commons gradually gained a control even over the executive power of the King, through the Cabinet system which grew up step by step under William, Anne and the first two Georges. All this was not foreseen by the men of 1689, whose intention was only to subject the kingly power to the bounds of law as defined by the parliamentary lawyers. But the Hanoverian Constitution of Walpole and the Pitts grew straight out of the Revolution Settlement by the logic of experience.

The Revolution has been branded as aristocratic. It was effected by the whole nation, by a union of all classes; but in a society still mainly agricultural, where the economic and social structure rendered the landlords the natural and accepted leaders of the countryside, noblemen and squires like the Tories Danby and Seymour, the Whigs Devonshire and Shrewsbury took the lead when resistance to government had to be improvised. The nation indeed recognized no other chiefs through whom it could act in such an emergency. A similar aristocratic and squirearchical leadership of the country had organized both the Roundhead and Cavalier armies at the beginning of the Civil War; it had, indeed, been partially eclipsed during the rule of Cromwell's military saints, but had been fully re-established at the Restoration of 1660. It continued after 1689 as before, and would in any case have continued until the Industrial Revolution gradually raised up a new social order. Even Despotism, if James had succeeded in setting it up, must in that age have governed through nobles and squires. James attempted to use the lords and country gentlemen who were the Lieutenants and

J.P.'s of their counties as the instruments of his Catholicizing policy, but they, like everyone else, turned against him. Having no other bureaucracy through which to work, he fell.

So far, the Revolution was indeed a demonstration of the power of the landlord classes, Whig and Tory alike. They were politically powerful because in the then formation of English Society they were indispensable. Any form of English government must in those days have worked through them.

The Revolution did quite as much for the legal, mercantile and popular elements in our national life as for the aristocratic or squirearchical. The worst permanent result of the Revolution was not the alleged increase in the power of the aristocracy but the undue conservatism that continued throughout the whole eighteenth century. The result of the reaction against James II's innovations was to put too great a stress, for many years to come, on the perpetuation of institutions in their existing form. James, in the interest of Roman Catholicism and Despotism, had remodelled the Town Corporations, invaded the liberties of the Universities and of the Church, and attempted to pack the House of Commons. In the rebound, the Ministries and Parliaments of the Eighteenth century feared to reform the Corporations, Universities, Church benefices and Parliamentary Constituencies, even in the interest of purer and more efficient government. James had treated charters as waste paper, so the men of the eighteenth century regarded the sheepskin with superstitious reverence. They held that whatever is is right—if it can show a charter. The hundred and fifty years that followed the Revolution are the most conservative in our annals though by no means the least free, happy or prosperous.

The Whig Governments before Burke, and the Tory Governments after him, all had too much reverence for the letter of the Revolution Settlement. It became a flag of ultraconservatism, first Whig, then Tory. To Walpole, Blackstone, Burke, Eldon and the anti-Jacobin Tories of the early nineteenth century, the year 1689 seemed the last year of creation, when God looked upon England and saw that it was good.

But when this ultraconservative mood at length passed away, the bases of the Revolution Settlement still remained as the foundations of the new era of rapid Reform, in which we are still living after more than a hundred years. The relation of the Crown to Parliament and to the Law; the independence of Judges; the annual meeting of Parliament; the financial supremacy of the Commons; the position of the Church of England; the Toleration of religious Dissent; freedom of political speech and writing subject to no control but the opinion of a jury; in short a Constitutional Monarchy for a free people, these are the bases of our polity and they were well and truly laid by the Whigs and Tories, the nobles, squires, lawyers, merchants and populace who rose up against James II.

But unless strength upholds the free, freedom cannot live. And the Revolution Settlement gave us strength as well as freedom. The Marlborough wars soon demonstrated that; and England was never so safe and so powerful as in the eighteenth century, especially after the Parliamentary Union with Scotland, made in 1707, had united the whole island of Britain "on a Revolution basis."

Between the death of Elizabeth and the Revolution of 1688, the constant struggle between Parliament and King had rendered England weak in the face of the world, except during the few years when Cromwell had given her strength at a heavy price. Our civil broils had occupied our energies and attention; sometimes both the King and the statesmen of the Opposition were pensioners of France; always Parliament had been chary of supply to governments whose policy they could not continuously control. In the reigns of the Jameses and Charleses, foreign countries had regarded our Parliament as a source of weakness, hampering the executive power: the Constitution of England was contemptuously compared to that of Poland.

But after the Revolution the world began to see that our parliamentary government, when fully established, was capable of becoming a source of national strength. Supplies that had been refused to Kings whom the Commons could not trust, were lavished on Ministries that had the confidence of the House. The money must be voted afresh annually, not granted for the King's life; and the Commons must see to its appropriation. On these strict conditions, the governments of William, Anne and the Georges had the run of the national purse such as their predecessors had not enjoyed. Moreover, the "Revolution Governments" had the confidence of the City as well as of Parliament. The system of loans based on taxes gave England the key to power. It was "Revolution finance" and Revolution policy that enabled Marlborough to defeat the Grand Monarch, when free government and religious toleration triumphed over the revoker of the Edict of Nantes. As a result of that victory, the European philosophers of the eighteenth century turned against political despotism and religious intolerance as causes of national weakness, and proclaimed to the world the peculiar merits of England's "happy constitution in Church and State."

Speaking of the wars of William and Anne, and more generally of the eighteenth century, Professor G. N. Clark writes:

"In France and Prussia and almost everywhere militarism and autocracy went hand in hand, but what enabled Britain to deploy its strength was the Revolution Settlement. The main lines of policy were laid down by a small gathering of Ministers who had at their disposal full departmental information about foreign affairs, finance, military and naval preparations and trade. By means of Parliament the Ministers brought into the service of that policy the wealth and manpower of the nation. . . . Parliament was a meeting-place where divergent economic interests were reconciled and combined so as to provide an adequate body of support for the government of the day."

In this way Britain obtained, not only political and religious liberty, but national power, greater than that of the unlimited monarchy of France. Such are the reasons why modern historians regard the Revolution a turning-point in the history of our country and of the world. . . .

The liberal-conservative character of the Revolution Settlement must be sought in the character of the House of Commons elected in January 1689. How and in what spirit was that House chosen? What, if any, were the instructions given to its members by their constituents?

The elections to the Convention Parliament took place under abnormal conditions. There was no King and no regular government. The country was in the greatest danger of internal convulsion and foreign conquest, and the national crisis loomed larger in men's minds than the usual Whig and Tory nonsense. An anxious, sober patriotism was the spirit of the hour. Moreover, the Whigs and Tories had for some time past been acting together as one party against James and had not yet had time to fly asunder and resume their old quarrels. . . .

The first business of the Convention was to decide who should fill the throne, and on that issue the new Whig and the new Tory parties came into existence. Yet the differences of parties on the dynastic question arose from a difference of theory rather than of practice. Both sides desired William to stay in England as head of the administration. The question in dispute was by what right and with what title he should bear rule.

The Tory politicians and the Anglican clergy in Charles II's reign had pledged themselves repeatedly to the theory of divine hereditary right of Kings and non-resistance of subjects. They had since been compelled to resist James II, in spite of all their theories, because they were men. But also because they were men, they could not all of them at once abandon the whole set of associated ideas in which they had been brought up. They could not, as quickly as the Vicar of Bray, treat "passive obedience as a jest" and make "a joke of non-resistance." They set themselves therefore to explain away the Revolution while reaping its fruits in practice. They desired to make such a settlement of the Crown as would not be in too obvious contradiction of the doctrines which they had all so recently proclaimed, and which many of them still loved and reverenced. They asserted, to begin with, that James had never been driven away, but that he had voluntarily deserted his functions. They had risen against him in arms, meaning only to bring him to reason, and he had, instead of submitting, fled oversea to the national enemy. The blessed word "abdicate" would save his subjects from the sin of having deposed him. James had "abdicated" the government. And further, the Tories hoped that a little ingenuity could surely be used to avoid a breach in the divinely appointed order of hereditary succession.

Such was the nature of Tory anxieties when the Convention met in January 1689.

The Whigs, on the other hand, thought that a slight change in the order of succession would be a good thing in itself, because it would kill the Stuart theory of divine hereditary right. It would make the title to the Crown a Parliamentary title, to the same extent as in Plantagenet and Tudor days, when Parliament had several times disposed of the Crown, not always to the nearest of kin. The Whigs believed that such another Parliamentary gift of the Crown would establish their own theory of the contract between King and People, involving the forfeiture of the Crown in case of breach of that contract. Only so, thought the Whigs, could the limited nature of the monarchy be secured for all time. No doubt the Tories of 1689, like the Cavaliers of 1640 and 1660, wished the powers of the Crown to be limited in practice. But was such a Constitutional practice consonant with a theory suited only to despotism? For if the King continued, in the eyes of half his subjects, to hold a quasi-divine office by inheritance, how was a mere earthly Parliament to limit his supernatural rights whenever he chose to insist on them? A divine monarchy must always override a mere human Parliament. Since monarchy and Parliament could not both be divine in men's eyes, let them both, said the Whigs, be human, and here is our great opportunity to make them so. . . .

One important concession was made to the Tory view. James was declared to have "abdicated" the government by his voluntary flight. He was not declared to have been "deposed," nor to have "forfaulted," that is "forfeited," the Crown as the Scottish Convention at Edinburgh pronounced, in its more thorough-going Whig manner. . . .

The Commons' formula, to which the Lords finally agreed, ran as follows:

"That King James the Second, having endeavoured to subvert the Constitution of the Kingdom, by breaking the *Original Contract* between King and people [a Whig remark], and by the advice of Jesuits and other wicked persons having violated the fundamental laws and withdrawn himself out of the Kingdom, hath *abdicated* the government [a concession to the Tories] and that *the throne is thereby vacant*" [a Whig conclusion]. . . .

William and Mary were not made King and Queen without conditions. The instrument by which the Convention raised them to the throne was the famous Declaration of Right. It made a long recital of the various illegal acts of James, more especially his claim to suspend the laws by Prerogative; it declared all these actions to have been illegal, and it required the acceptance of these limitations of the royal power by the new sovereigns as a condition of their elevation to the throne.

. . . An agreed contract was freely made between Crown and people which prevented for all time to come a repetition of the tragedies of the Stuart Kings. The pendulum-swing of alternate violence of rebels and royalists was slowed down to the gentler oscillation of rival Parliamentary parties. And what the Crown lost in power it gained in security. The Republican movement was buried, not to revive in England in any formidable manner either at the time of the French Revolution, or with the coming of social democracy in the nineteenth and twentieth centuries. England had acquired the outline of a Constitution in which she could work out her remoter destinies. . . .

The fundamental question at issue in 1688 had been this—Is the law above the King, or is the King above the law? The interest of Parliament was identified with that of the law, because, undoubtedly, Parliament could alter the law. It followed that, if law stood above the King's will, yet remained alterable by Parliament, Parliament would be the supreme power in the State.

James II attempted to make the law alterable wholesale by the King. This, if it had been permitted, must have made the King supreme over Parliament, and, in fact, a despot. The events of the winter of 1688–9 gave the victory to the opposition idea, which Chief Justice Coke and Selden had enunciated early in the century, that the King was the chief servant of the law, but not its master; the executant of the law, not its source; the laws should only be alterable by Parliament—Kings, Lords and Commons together. It is this that makes the Revolution the decisive event in the history of the English Constitution. It was decisive because it was never undone, as most of the work of the Cromwellian Revolution had been undone.

It is true that the first Civil War had been fought partly on this same issue:— the Common Law in league with Parliament had, on the field of Naseby, triumphed over the King in the struggle for the supreme place in the Constitution. But the victory of Law and Parliament had, on that occasion, been won only because

Puritanism, the strongest religious passion of the hour, had supplied the fighting force. And religious passion very soon confused the Constitutional issue. Puritanism burst the legal bounds and, coupled with militarism, overthrew law and Parliament as well as King. Hence the necessity of the restoration in 1660 of King, law and Parliament together, without any clear definition of their ultimate mutual relations.

Now, in this second crisis of 1688, law and Parliament had on their side not only the Puritan passion, which had greatly declined, but the whole force of Protestant-Anglicanism, which was then at its height, and the rising influence of Latitudinarian scepticism—all arrayed against the weak Roman Catholic interest to which James had attached the political fortunes of the royal cause. The ultimate victor of the seventeenth-century struggle was not Pym or Cromwell, with their Puritan ideals, but Coke and Selden with their secular idea of the supremacy of law. In 1689 the Puritans had to be content with a bare toleration. But law triumphed, and therefore the law-making Parliament triumphed finally over the King. . . .

The ultimate view that we take of the Revolution of 1688 must be determined by our preference either for royal absolutism or for parliamentary government. James II forced England to choose once for all between these two: he refused to inhabit any halfway house. It was as well that the choice had to be made so decisively and so soon; for the compromise system of the Restoration, though very useful in its day, had led to weakness abroad and constant strife at home.

The system of government by discussion has its disadvantages, under which in new forms we are labouring to-day, in face of absolutist governments of a new and more formidable type than those of Europe of the *ancien régime*. But if, on the balance, we prefer the path on which our feet are planted, we must commend the choice that was made once for all at the English Revolution.

The Revolution as a Reinforcement
of English Institutions

DAVID OGG

David Ogg, born in 1887, has been a frequent visitor to this country. His first major work was *Europe in the Seventeenth Century* (1925), followed nine years later by his two-volume *England in the Reign of Charles II*. Since 1959 he has been Honorary Fellow of New College, Oxford. The following selection is taken from the work which completes his great study of the later seventeenth century.

ONE of the best sources for the study of the English Revolution is to be found in the proclamations and declarations put forth by the contestants; never before had the printed word played such a part in political events. On 17 October 1688 James issued a proclamation for the restoration of the corporations, and the removal therefrom of those who had been intruded; three days later came his proclamation ordering a strict watch to be kept on the coasts, and forbidding the spread of false news. On 1 November, the eve of his embarkation, there was an announcement from the prince of Orange, giving his reasons for invading England; next day, James imposed a ban on all public announcements made by the prince. On 6 November the king, after referring to the invasion, promised redress of all grievances; on the 17th a third party—the Lords—intervened with a declaration announcing that war could be avoided only by the speedy summoning of parliament. Then, on 22 November, there were published announcements, from the nobility, gentry, and commonalty of York and Nottingham,

declaring adhesion to the prince of Orange; and, at last, on 30 November, a royal proclamation intimated a meeting of parliament for the 15th of January. The conditions laid down by William at Hungerford were published on 9 December; two days later, James, announcing that he had been forced to send his queen and son to safety, confessed that, as he could not trust the army, he would offer no opposition to the prince. On the same day the lords spiritual and temporal, in and about the cities of London and Westminster, intimated that, as the king had withdrawn himself, they had applied to the prince to summon a free parliament, with liberty of conscience to Protestant Dissenters. This date, 11 December, marked the end of the reign of James II and the beginning of the interregnum.

The literary duel continued throughout the interregnum. During his short stay at Rochester James, on 22 December, put forth a proclamation intimating that he had left Whitehall because of the discourteous conduct of the prince, but he would return at the call of the nation, whenever it agreed to have liberty of conscience. This

From David Ogg, *England in the Reigns of James II and William III* (Oxford, 1955). Reprinted by permission of the Clarendon Press, Oxford, pp. 222–223, 225–226, 231–233, 235–239, 242–245, 486–488, 498, 508–509, 547.

coincided with an order from the Lords, assembled in their House, requiring all papists to leave London. Next day, 23 December, the prince of Orange summoned all persons who had served in any of Charles II's parliaments to meet at St. James's on the 26th, together with the lord mayor, aldermen, and fifty of the common council of the city of London. These informal assemblies of Lords, ex-Commons, and city magistrates asked William to summon a convention. On Christmas Day the lords spiritual and temporal requested the prince of Orange to take upon himself the direction of affairs until the meeting of the intended convention on 22 January, for which His Highness was asked to direct the issue of writs. His compliance with this request was announced on 29 December. Finally, on 4 January 1689, came a proclamation from James, in the form of a letter to the privy council, intimating the concessions which he had made, and announcing to the world that he had been obliged to leave his country because of his fear of death. The history of the Revolution can be little more than comment on these official pronouncements.

If it be granted that the model revolution is one that avoids bloodshed and maintains a fundamental continuity with the past, then the English Revolution was a model of its kind. Parliament was not in session, but a body of lords and bishops sat in their House, while old parliamentarians met at St. James's, each of which conclaves invited William to assume the administration. The ex-Commons sitting at St. James's had, of course, no official status, but the lords spiritual and temporal, though consisting only of "those about London and Westminster," and though not summoned by a king, had a somewhat stronger position, because they were independent of election. Indeed, they acted in an executive capacity; that they should have done so is one of the many illustrations of the aristocratic character both of the English constitution and of the English revolution. . . .

The Commons were the first to address themselves to the great constitutional questions raised by recent events; and, as there was a certain hesitancy on the part of new members, the lead was taken by such veterans as Colonel Birch, Sir T. Clarges, and Sergeant Maynard, with the help of those experienced parliamentarians Sir T. Lee, Sir T. Littleton, and Sir Edward Seymour. Birch, who had started life as a carter, had a habit of driving straight through the subtleties and fine distinctions of debate. "These forty years," he declared, "we have been striving against anti-Christ, popery and tyranny." Here was an echo of a far-off past; this link with the Puritan Revolution was evidenced by the passing, on 29 January, of a resolution that a Popish prince was inconsistent with a Protestant state. There was another reminiscence, this time of the Restoration, in Lord Falkland's proposal that, before they filled the throne, they should resolve what powers were to be conferred on the ruler, a proposal which started a hubbub of suggestions—frequent parliaments, independent judges, inviolability of corporations, and many more. That these demands were placed in the forefront may be attributed in part to the influence of Halifax, who was the reputed author of a broadsheet, distributed among the Commons, which counselled them to agree on their constitution before they decided on their governor. So the House resolved that, before proceeding to fill the throne, it would secure the religion, laws, and liberties of the nation. The mistake of 1660 would not be made a second time. . . .

As the Restoration had been followed by an attempt to grant toleration to Protestant Dissenters, so the Revolution raised again the great question of unity within the Protestant fold. Ever since 1679, and even more in the reign of James II, it had been realized that the Protestant Dissenters had been thrown, by the menace of popery, into the same camp as the Anglicans; and to many it seemed that, politically at least, the two had much in common; there was also the example of Scotland, where the Presbyterians had maintained the most consistent opposition to the later Stuarts. Not unnaturally, therefore, it was from the period of the Popish Plot that two abortive measures, a Toleration Bill and a Comprehension Bill were revived. Nottingham tried to secure the passage of both Bills. He had little difficulty with the first, but he failed with the second, the more ambitious of the two. This, the Comprehension Bill, would have relaxed the ritual and discipline of the church of England in such a manner that Nonconformists might attend the parish church without violation of their scruples against such practices as kneeling, and wearing the surplice. It would also have qualified for the cure of souls all Dissenters who took the oath against transubstantiation, and expressed approval of the doctrine, worship, and government of the church of England. But the strong church party in the Commons successfully opposed the Bill, which was dropped on 8 April. The argument had prevailed that, as Convocation was about to be summoned, to that body should be referred the great questions raised by the problem of establishing unity in non-Catholic England.

Another abortive proposal at this time showed how a section, at least of the Convention, was anxious to mitigate the rigidity of the old religious distinctions, and to end the monopoly whereby office holding was limited to Anglicans. At the third reading in the Lords of the Bill for substituting new oaths for the old oaths of allegiance and supremacy (23 March), one of the peers offered as a rider a clause which would have qualified for office anyone who had taken the sacrament either according to the practice of the church of England, or according to that of any recognized Protestant communion. The rider was lost. Those who protested against this rejection gave reasons which show a remarkable advance on contemporary opinion. By the rejection of the proposal, maintained the protesting minority, a great part of the Protestant freemen of England were excluded from public employment "from a mere scruple of conscience"; moreover, these men professed doctrines which were about to be publicly tolerated in a Bill then before the House (the Toleration Bill). This exclusion, contended the protesting peers, might have bad effects on Protestant and Reformed churches abroad, because it turned the edge of a law, intended to penalize Papists, against Protestants and friends of the government as settled by the Revolution. Lastly, in the words of this protest, "mysteries of religion and divine worship are of divine original, and of a nature so wholly distinct from the secular affairs of politic society that they cannot be applied to these ends." In these words, the spirit of 1689 anticipated that of 1829.

It was very different with the Toleration Bill. This did not abolish any of the penal statutes against Protestant Dissenters, but merely declared that they should not be enforced against those who fulfilled certain conditions. These conditions included, for laymen, the new oaths of fidelity to William and Mary, and the standard oath against transubstantiation; for preachers there was added the requirement of subscription to the Thirty-nine Articles, except those relating to homilies, traditions of the church, and consecration of bishops. Some recognition of the status of dissenting ministers (qualified as above) was conceded by their exemption from parish offices and from serving on juries; but no exemption from tithe was given, and it was expressly declared that nothing in the Act was intended to give relief to Roman Catholics. No longer were dissenting meetings to be held behind closed doors; indeed, their places of worship were to be certified to the bishop or archdeacon of the diocese. . . .

The coronation of William and Mary took place on 11 April with the customary pageantry. In the absence of Sancroft, Compton officiated, and Mary was crowned as queen regnant. In accordance with the Act for establishing the coronation oath, the two sovereigns were obliged to swear that they would govern the people of England and the dominions thereto belonging according to "the statutes in parliament agreed upon, and the laws and customs of the same"; that they would maintain the true profession of the Gospel, and "the Protestant Reformed Religion established by law." Two new things had thus been introduced into the coronation oath, namely, the statutes of parliament, and the "Protestant Reformed Religion." In regard to the first, kings had formerly been obliged to swear observance of the laws and customs emanating from their royal predecessors, especially those granted to the clergy by St. Edward. These are now replaced by the laws and statutes of the realm.

Coronation oaths, though so few in number, are the most precious of all the materials on which the constitutional historian has to work, because they embody fundamental conceptions of the state; they are sensitive to deep-seated changes in these conceptions, and they are sworn in circumstances of the utmost solemnity. Conversely, their misinterpretation, as by George III, may prove of momentous consequence; indeed, if that monarch or his advisers had read the debates in the Commons on the new oath, they would have seen that it was not intended to bind the king in his legislative capacity, for the legislature had in view the fact that important concessions in religious matters were being embodied in Bills, to which it was hoped that the crown would assent. Some of the essential principles of both the Revolution and the modern constitution were incorporated in the coronation oath, almost as much as in the Bill of Rights; but the former is much more difficult of interpretation, because so much shorter, and because, even within its brevity, there appears on modern standards to be redundance. About one newcomer we can be certain—the king is no longer the sole law-giver, for thenceforward he is only a part of the legislative body; here is an obvious and noncontroversial change. But it is otherwise with the second newcomer —"the Protestant Reformed Religion established by law." Here the main difficulty arises from its context, since it immediately precedes the obligation to defend the settlement of the church of England and Ireland, "as by law established." Does this imply that "the Protestant Reformed Religion established by law" was something different from the doctrine and discipline of the church of England, also established by law? This question was in the mind of one parliamentarian when he objected that the new phrase created another church in addition to the church of England; moreover, the amended formula "Protestant Church of England" was rejected by the House. So the two apparently similar things were kept apart. Nor is this the end of the supposed redundance, for nowadays "Protestant" and "Reformed" are regarded as meaning exactly the same thing, and it has even been held that to distinguish between the two is mere pedantry.

But before we dismiss the new coronation oath as a piece of pedantry or redundance, we should bear in mind that tautology is often the resort of those who are striving desperately to be clear and emphatic; also, that words which mean the same thing today have not always meant the same thing. Nor was the coronation oath enunciated, as it were, *in vacuo;* on the contrary, it was closely related to historical events, and can be understood only in the light of these events. Unlike previous coronation oaths, this one was drafted by laymen, to be understood by laymen. The legislators provided a guarantee for the church of England, but, on the other hand, they kept in view the part played by that church in recent history, and how, by its insistence on Divine Right and Nonresistance, it had, in their opinion, done much to encourage the excesses of the Stuarts. So long as the Stuarts had supported the established church, they were free to engage in a policy of crypto- or public Catholicism; and so it seemed to many intelligent laymen that the church of England had degenerated from the position of a national church into that of a political party. The Seven Bishops had for a time restored this lost prestige, but only for a time, because five of them refused to recognize William; it was also clear that the church was divided, or at best only lukewarm in the cause of the Revolution. Accordingly, guarantee of the church of England was preceded by guarantee of something else—the Protestant Reformed Religion. The legislators of 1689 were taking no risks.

This dual phrase also derived from the past. By 1689 the term "Protestant" was coming to be used in its modern sense as an inclusive term for all the western churches opposed to Rome; but it was still distinguished from "Reformed," that is, the more extreme Calvinist and Zwinglian movements of the later sixteenth century which had exercised such influence on the England of Elizabeth. Already the Whigs had emphasized the glories of Elizabeth's reign in contrast with the shame of the Stuarts; and, as that shame deepened, many Englishmen—not necessarily Whigs, for this was well above party distinction—reverted to those great changes of the sixteenth century which, in their view, had created a "Protestant" and "Reformed" England. By "Reformed" they meant the Elizabethan settlement, when some of the most characteristic doctrines of Calvinism had been embodied in the Thirty-nine Articles, where they still remain. Here was a "Reformed" religion, "established by law"; or, in other words, a reminder that if the church of England had thoughts of taking the path to Rome, it had not yet (so far as the law was concerned) retraced the steps already taken on the way to Geneva. To most churchmen this reminder was obnoxious in the extreme.

"Reformed" was preceded by "Protestant." Here there is great latitude of interpretation. The term may possibly have been used in order to exclude the casuist who could argue that, after the Council of Trent, the church of Rome was a "Reformed" church; or it may have been adopted simply as the widest possible expression to denote those churches of western Europe which were uncompromisingly opposed to Rome. The term, described in the debates as an "honourable" one, may have included both these things; but it may also have had some reference to Henry VIII's Reformation, with its transference of enormous areas of church lands to secular proprietors, many of them among the ancestors of those who adopted the phrase; indeed, Henry's Reformation was distinctively "Protestant" in the sense that the German or Lutheran reformers had used the word, since their original "protest" was not merely against certain Roman Catholic practices, but against the threat of imperial interference with large-scale confiscations of land. Now Henry's confiscations had also been authorized by law; here was the security by which many members of parliament held their estates. So there was no redundance or pedantry in adding "Protestant" to "Reformed," for these words meant quite different things. Taking the Henrician with the Elizabethan settlement, the view of parliament was that the official religion of England, *as recognized by law,* was both Protestant and Reformed.

These technical matters should not conceal the national importance of what the Revolution government was trying, almost desperately, to do. It was emulating the example set in Elizabeth's reign, when the menace from Spain was countered by association with those Protestant and Reformed communities on the continent which shared our peril; now that we were confronted by a similar menace from France, parliament clearly implied a renewal of this alignment with foreign churches again threatened by militant Catholicism, churches with which Anglicans indignantly repudiated any connexion. Nor was this all; for, so long as there remained any doubt whether or not England was Protestant, there was always a loophole for the intervention of the clergy in secular matters; whereas Protestantism (as distinct from the old "Reformed" doctrines) means erastianism, or the complete subordination of church to state. Archbishops and bishops would continue to sit in the Lords, as some of them sat for a time in the Cabinet; but in both capacities their position was public and responsible, not secret and irresponsible. Here indeed we have the central achievement of the Revolution; "this coronation oath," declared a member of the House, "is the very touchstone and symbol of your government"; because its dual phrase, so often misunderstood, or resented, or repudiated, has served to enunciate one of the essential characteristics of Anglo-Saxon civilization. The alternative was Bourbon-Stuart civilization, a totalitarian system, having as its agents the priest, the dragoon, and the hangman, a system to which many Englishmen were determined not to submit. It was in accordance with this determination that William III declared war on Louis XIV on 7 May 1689. . . .

The Bill of Rights is our greatest constitutional document since Magna Carta; and, like that document, it emanated from the misdeeds of a king. Both instruments were concerned, not to enunciate abstract principles of government, but to provide safeguards against royal wrongdoings, many of them specified. Some of the omissions from the Bill of Rights are of interest. Reference to the social contract had disappeared in the conferences between the two Houses in February; on the other hand, the whole measure implies some kind of contract between king and nation, based not on law, but on the "complete confidence" which parliament professed in the two sovereigns. There is little about parliament, except that it should be held frequently, and that elections should be free; otherwise, certain executive acts are pronounced legal only if parliament concurs. The suspending power is ruled out altogether; the dispensing power disappeared in a more devious way. At first,

it was declared invalid only "as it hath been exercised of late"; but a later clause (II) of the Bill enacted that no dispensation to a statute could be allowed unless expressly provided for in the statute itself, or in any statute passed by that session of parliament. As no such statute was passed, the royal exercise of the dispensing power came to an end.

Otherwise, there was no attempt to define the extent of the royal powers. The prerogative of mercy, the king's right to choose his ministers, to declare war and make peace—all these are left untouched. The legislators of 1689 did not even try to make monarchy foolproof; all that they were concerned with was that certain evils within their own experience should not recur. It is mainly for this reason that recent historians have depreciated the value of the Bill of Rights, arguing that it left William, as later George III, with many powers denied to the sovereigns of today. But this is to read the present into the past, and to misunderstand the essentially English character of the document. The Bill of Rights reaffirmed what had been asserted by the great medieval jurists, that the king is subject to law; and that, for many of his most important acts, there must be the consent of those (whether *magnates* or parliament) who could claim to speak on behalf of the nation. True, the king was left with certain important rights; but, meanwhile, parliament had come to stay, and it was only a matter of time before the residual prerogative of the king in person would yield to the rule of king in parliament.

In one more respect modern historiography has done less than justice to the Bill of Rights. With the discredit into which parliamentary institutions have fallen in some quarters, accentuated by assiduous eulogy of the Stuarts,* the Revolution has been hailed as a drab or "bourgeois" episode in our history, ending a period of "brilliant" court life, and ushering in an era of dull and not always intelligent kings. But, at least from the point of view of the common man, the advantage does not always lie with the country governed by a fascist ruler, however facetious or devout; indeed, it may be much more enjoyable to read about such kings than to live under them. It was just for these unspectacular, everyday conditions that the Bill of Rights provided. There was not a word about democracy, nor about the economic betterment of the people, nor about the extension of the franchise, but there was a great deal about those elementary legal rights of the subject, rights to which we are now so accustomed that we take them for granted, and therefore assume that they have never been threatened. It is in the guarantee of these rights that the value of the Revolution consists; nor does the fact that we have enjoyed them so long diminish the importance of their origin. "The Bill of Rights is to be as long as we are a nation," declared a member of the House of Commons, and he was not exaggerating.

Lastly, the Bill of Rights evoked from some contemporaries the opinion that it was only the beginning of far-reaching reform. There should, it was argued, be more guarantees for the rights of the subject, particularly in treason trials; the remedy of habeas corpus should be extended, and made more easily available. Most notable was the change in the practice and theory of the prerogative. The clemency of William's rule proved that for all, except the Jacobites, a policy of mercy was perfectly safe, and even the Jacobites were treated with great lenity. Moreover, William's practice was backed by a gradual change in public opinion, whereby the doctrine was repudiated that, for effective government, brutality was necessary. Here are the words of a contemporary, writing in 1692:

It is a great mistake to imagine that an easie and full power of chopping men in pieces upon a block, or confining them in Newgate or other gaols, can add any strength to the crown, for Englishmen, generally speaking, are fond of a king, not only for his, but for their own sakes. . . . No authority can be

so lasting as that which is founded on love and esteem.

Stuart England, like so many continental countries, had found kingship and liberty incompatible; the Revolution of 1688 gave us a constitution in which the two are inseparable. . . .

Sovereignty is one of the most obscure and debated of all political subjects, for hardly any two people can agree in defining either its source or its extent. But in the progress of English civilization one aspect of the problem, namely, legal or parliamentary sovereignty, has steadily acquired clarity of definition and latitude of application, so that today it is almost outside the realm of controversy.

As early as the thirteenth century Bracton had thought in terms of some kind of association for the purposes of government, composed of king and *magnates*; then Magna Carta had formulated the principle of no taxation without the consent of the *commune consilium regni*. A more advanced stage was that represented by Coke who, in his Fourth Institute, claimed that the power of parliament was "absolute and transcendent"; but his examples show that he had in mind the High Court of Parliament, concerned with the making of laws, rather than with the direction of policy. Next came Hobbes, whose theory of an unlimited, undivided sovereignty, though postulated of a single, hereditary personality, was easily applicable to a body of men, such as king in parliament, a theory so challenging and absolute as to repel all who thought in terms of balance or compromise, and all who resented the idea that government is ultimately dependent on force. Nevertheless, it was Hobbes's theory, the most logical and the most misunderstood of the century, that ultimately prevailed, though the achievement was indirect and long delayed. In the course of that process the Revolution of 1688 is the dividing line between two periods in the history of sovereignty—an earlier one, in which there was no guarantee for the summoning of parliament; and a later one, in which, though both Houses had an assured and permanent place, the king was still endowed with certain personal prerogatives which limited the scope of parliamentary sovereignty. Hence, in this later stage, it was natural for Locke to popularize at home, and even more abroad, the idea of division of powers, a cordial much more palatable than the distasteful medicine prescribed by Hobbes. But, even then, the formula of Hobbes was in process of application; for there was gradually emerging that omnipotent and indivisible trinity of King, Lords, and Commons in which supreme power and direction are vested today.

Accordingly, in any estimate of the progress made by parliamentary sovereignty in the later seventeenth century, a beginning must be made with those personal rights still exercised by the crown. These rights were legacies from a long and sacred past. The prerogative of the Stuarts had owed much to the sacerdotal element in kingship; and, whatever may be thought of Charles II's virtues, there can be no doubt that, in his exercise of one element in that prerogative—the healing touch—he was (therapeutically) by far the most efficacious of English kings. This literal contact with the body of the subject, never attempted by William, was practiced for the last time by queen Anne. In spite of the Bill of Rights, there still survived, in English kingship, many powers and exemptions, some of them relics of an older, mystic conception of sovereignty; for the prerogative was thought of as something essentially good, since it did not extend to anything that might injure the subject, or deprive him of his just rights. The king, it was conceived, had an interest in all his subjects, and a claim to their service; he had supreme patronage, appointing bishops by his nomination; as the fountain of honour, he created peers; as the supreme repository of mercy, he granted pardons. He could incorporate a town; and, in the opinion of some, he could revoke a grant of incorpora-

tion; he could make an alien free-born; he could put a value on the coin of the realm; he had a right to the lands of convicted felons. His prerogative was an essential part of the common law of England. Such were among the commonplaces of those lawyers who attempted to define this, the most elusive element in the constitution.

As James II had taken the Nonresistance divines too seriously, so he may have been encouraged, in his course of conduct, by the cloudy amplitude of rights and privileges with which the lawyers surrounded the throne. That cloudiness had been clarified in the Revolution settlement only by dispersal of the fog surrounding the dispensing power; otherwise, most of the old rights remained, including those of summoning, proroguing, and dissolving parliament; dismissing judges (before the Act of Settlement); appointing to high offices of state; vetoing legislation; declaring war and making peace. These were substantial rights. It is one of the paradoxes of English history that the parliamentary constitution dates from an Act which diminished the royal power so little, and from the rule of a king whose prerogatives were so great. . . .

It was by means of his moderate and reasonable use of such a vast prerogative that William helped to secure for the crown a permanent place in the British constitution. This is all the more remarkable as he was by nature autocratic and headstrong; but his great self-control kept these instincts within bounds. Almost unfettered by the letter of the constitution, he nevertheless respected its spirit. . . .

The first of these rights, that of summoning, proroguing, and dissolving parliament was limited generally by the clause in the Bill of Rights that, for the redress of grievances and the amending of the laws, "parliaments ought to be held frequently"; and, more specifically by the Triennial Act of 1694. This latter statute was modified by an Act of 1696, the year of the Jacobite Assassination Plot, which enacted that parliament should not determine by the death of the sovereign, but might sit for six months thereafter. These were the legislative measures which ensured for parliament a permanent place in the constitution, and so must be regarded as the most important element in the Revolution settlement.

It is in these measures, and in the debates to which they gave rise, that we can detect the most striking characteristic of parliament, namely, the gradual adaptation of a medieval institution to more modern needs. . . .

This book has attempted, in its references to society and institutions, to connect the development of English civilization with the gradual and peaceful adaptation of medieval survivals; in illustration of this development, the examples of crown and parliament may be cited. In parliament, even as late as the end of the seventeenth century, the Lords, in this little distinguishable from the feudal magnates, still exercised personal privileges which we would consider social abuses; while the Commons were returned by methods, few of which would be commended by the political theorist of today. In both Houses there were thus traces of a perverted medievalism. Nevertheless, parliament had now become permanent and national, directing the state through its first European war, and committing it to another, in which the foundations of world supremacy were to be laid. A similar process of adaptation can be seen in the changed place assigned to the crown in our constitution; and, in the functions now performed by the king, it is possible to detect the sublimated relics of ancient party aspiration. On the one hand, the old Whig, applying his common law maxim to the prerogative, would acclaim in the sovereign such absolute detachment from party distinction and political initiative as to make public wrongdoing impossible; on the other hand, the old Tory, his religion transmuted into a sentiment, would applaud in the same sovereign a human link, binding together a great commonwealth of free nations, a ruler far more potent than any Divine Right king. Thus the monarchy is the most remarkable of all these survivals because, while its powers are still regulated by a medieval fiction, it has been adapted to conditions undreamed of in the past. . . .

The art of living together in society is one of the most difficult of all arts, and history is strewn with the wreckage of failures to achieve it. To us, the Revolution of 1688 and the establishment of a Protestant, maritime state may well seem remote, as the thought of Locke may seem trite or commonplace; the first to be taken for granted, the second in danger of depreciation, because anyone can understand it. We may have outgrown these things, but nevertheless they have determined the evolution of Anglo-Saxon civilization in two hemispheres, maintained by communities which are as ready to defend their liberties as they are unwilling to enforce them on others. This voluntary element, this aversion from proselytism and propaganda, this spirit of live and let live is our most precious heritage from the seventeenth century. That its exponents still survive the threats of intolerance and repression is the distinctive achievement which unites the English-speaking world.

PART III: RECENT ANTI–WHIG REVISIONS AND RESTORATIONS

Were the Jacobites Right?

GEORGE L. CHERRY

George L. Cherry was born in 1905. He received his graduate training at Northwestern University from which he received his doctorate in 1938. During the war he served with the Air Force, and after his tour of duty, returned to teaching. Currently, he is Associate Professor of History at the University of Southern Illinois. He has devoted most of his attention to monographic studies on the reign of William and Mary.

THE mosaic of political concepts advanced during the interregnum for the settlement of the English government has remained incompletely constructed. This deficiency has resulted largely from three factors. In the first place, the Whig foundations of the arrangement have received greater emphasis than the alternative proposals. The Whig concepts sounded the death knell to absolutism and provided for the beginnings of a limited monarchy, under which form of government England was to rise to new heights of wealth, power, and prestige. To emphasize the principles that seemingly motivated this startling development would therefore be natural. In the second place, writers have considered the discussions of the interregnum, and particularly the debates in the Convention Parliament, less important than the philosophy of John Locke, who wrote after the settlement, or that of Filmer and Harrington, who wrote before the revolution. A typical disparaging analysis of the Convention deliberations is given by the historian James Ralph: "The whole Dispute about the Words abdicate, desert, and vacancy, was fitter for a School than a House of Parliament, and might have been expected in some Assembly of Pedants." Subsequent authors have but little altered the opinion of Ralph. Some of them have paraphrased the major speeches; others have given almost no attention to the discussions; a few have omitted them entirely. All of them have neglected to reveal the pattern of political concepts. In the third place, Jacobite ideas have received no special attention. This omission resulted from the unpopularity of these concepts and the belief that Jacobitism from the beginning was a lost cause. But Jacobitism did exist.

The importance of Jacobitism as a political force for the half-century after the revolution warrants an investigation of its foundations. At the time of James's first flight, the party consisted largely of Catholics. The nucleus grew when the captured

From George L. Cherry, "The Legal and Philosophical Position of the Jacobites, 1688–1689," *Journal of Modern History,* vol. XXII, No. 4, December, 1950, pp. 309–321. Reprinted by permission of the University of Chicago Press.

59

king was returned to London. This group was increased by the action of William when he forced the king out of England. During the election in January 1689 the Jacobite faction was one of the groups to compete for Convention seats. The party was much larger than was generally supposed. When the Convention met, 200 of the 513 members had served in the parliament of 1685. The fight in the commons for retaining James in some status was led by Lord Charles Fanshaw, Sir Christopher Musgrave, Sir Edward Seymour, and Mr. Heneage Finch. When the resolution on the vacancy was brought before the house, 151 members voted in the negative. In the upper chamber Jacobite strength was greater. On the question of the regency 49 peers voted for retaining James, while 51 voted against him. Among the leaders supporting the regency were the Earls of Clarendon, Rochester, and Nottingham; Sidney Godolphin, baron of Rialton; the Bishop of Ely; and the Archbishop of York. These lords were vigorous in their opposition to the commons action until the final decision on the "vacancy" resolution was reached. On this question 45 lords voted nay, and 39 of the peers entered their protests. Those figures give evidence of the strength of the group in the Convention. During the remainder of the Stuart period probably no fewer than fifty Jacobites held seats in parliament. These leaders worked actively for the restoration of the old order, while the majority of the party remained aloof from the government and engaged in plots for the return of James or his heirs. "Jacobitism remained a serious and powerful political cause until 1746." In view of the significance of Jacobitism, its concepts will be presented in this article through an analysis of Jacobite ideas on the following topics: the institutional authority to solve the constitutional problem; the divine-right theory; the compact theory; the plan for a regency; the royal hereditary rights; the abdication principle; and the vacancy of the throne.

An important question under discussion

during the interregnum was the authority of the English institutions, in the absence of the king, to settle the constitutional crisis created by the flight of James II. The Jacobites maintained that the Convention was without legal authority to make the settlement through a breach of the line of succession. . . .

The flight initiated the second phase of the problem of stabilizing the English government. In this phase the government was operating without a king and there was danger of the governmental balance being upset. During this period a temporary expedient was advanced by the lords and commons who had served in the parliaments of Charles II. The lords, who considered the possible alternatives, had been urged by Lord William Pagett to declare the king's withdrawal a demise and to select Mary as queen. The motion was not carried because of the vigorous opposition of the Earls of Pembroke and Nottingham. Two days later the prince asked the group to suggest ways and means for implementing his declaration to preserve the institutions of England. At this meeting of the delegates the body asked the prince to take charge of the government and to issue a call for a convention. In spite of the majority decision, the opinion was widely held that the convention would have no power to deal with the crisis because a legislature was without authority when the king did not participate. Although some of the leaders favored inviting James to return, provided that he would make certain guarantees, the clergy generally favored a regency through which a parliament could be called within the limits of the constitution. The apprehension of the Jacobite leaders was aroused by these developments. In a discussion of the implications with the Earl of Clarendon, Pembroke argued that in the approaching convention strenuous efforts must be made to guarantee the safety of James's interest while the political settlement was designed.

The third phase of the crisis developed during the meeting of the Convention.

During this period the Jacobites were working to prevent what they considered to be an illegal legislature from jeopardizing the traditional balance of the constitution. When the Convention met there was much discussion about the authority of the body to deal with the critical problem. First came the question about the seat of authority after the king had fled. Some observers agreed with a pamphleteer who analyzed the departure of the king as a dissolution of the government when he wrote, "If the Departure of the King amounts to such a Desertion as dissolves the Government, then the Power must necessarily revert and vest in the People, who may erect a new one, either according to the old *Model,* if they like it so well, or any other that they like and approve better." On the other hand, Nottingham expressed the belief that precedent gave the peers of the realm considerable authority under these circumstances: "In the absence of the King . . . I would not be understood to say, the government devolved upon the Lords; but I may say they are the government's great council in the interval of Parliaments, and may have greater sway by the privilege of their birth, in the exigencies of state: As appears in several instances, and particularly the first of *Henry* the sixth, and during his infancy." Deeper legal implications were seen, however, in the query put by Sir Christopher Musgrave to the legislative body. He said, "I would be clear whether the intent is to depose the King; if he has forfeited his Inheritance to the Crown, I would know from the Long Robe whether you can depose the King or no." This led to doubts as to the authority of the Convention to settle the question. It was emphasized that a convention was not a body that could be compared with a parliament. Because the king's writs had not been used to summon the body, it could have no legislative powers. Further clarifying the status of the Convention, one of the lords said, "As our Laws stand; We have misled a legal and free Parliament, and have got a Convention that cannot make Laws, nor call a Parliament that can, but what will need a confirmation from a better authority."

Referring to legal precedents in his interpretation of the authority, the Bishop of Ely recalled that the heir to the throne had been set aside by parliament on previous occasions. The bishop emphasized, however, that it did not follow "that every breach of the first original contract, gives us power to dispose of the lineal succession." This position was generally supported by the clergy, who were apprehensive about recognizing deposing powers. The spokesman for the group, Ely, gave a more complete analysis of the authority of parliament. Relating the powers of parliament to the original compact, he asserted that through this agreement the king and parliament had the authority to make and amend laws. Since the law of succession was a part of the compact, the powers of parliament did not include dealing with the crown until all heirs had abdicated. He doubted whether the precedents on the interruptions of the throne provided power to set aside the lineal succession because of the allegiance laws enacted under Elizabeth and James I. Since these laws were a part of the contract, parliament could not alter the succession except through the regular legislative process. Thus the Jacobites concluded that the Convention had no power to deal with the constitutional crisis. In spite of the solid legal foundations of their arguments, the Whig majority pushed ahead to settle the government. The widespread discussions during the interregnum defined many ideas on the nature of government; among them were those relating to the divine-right theory.

It was assumed during the eighteenth century that the Jacobites believed in "dispensing Power in the Crown, with indefeasible Hereditary Right, *Jure Divino.*" This idea has persisted for over two centuries. In his recent article about the revolution J. L. Duncan wrote: "On the one hand were ranged all believers in political absolutism, who then maintained that the King virtually stood above all law and reigned by virtue of divine right. His actions were regarded as sacrosanct and unchallengeable by any subject. In particular it was held that no circumstances could ever arise which would justify a subject in resisting by armed force any dictate of sovereign power." The evidence, however, does not support these positions. The facts reveal that, while the settlement was being accomplished, the majority of the Jacobites exchanged the divine-right theory of the Cavaliers for the more rational compact idea based on the precedents of constitutional growth. Some of the former remained, however, expressing themselves in letters, speeches, and pamphlets. A few of them believed in political absolutism, maintaining that the king was above the law and reigned by divine sanction. The most significant proponent of these ideas was James II, who wrote to the lords from Saint-Germain-en-Laye: "No change of fortune shall ever make Us forget Ourselves so far as to condescend to anything unbecoming that high and royall station on which God Almighty has by right of succession placed us." This position, however, was not widely accepted in official circles. During the Convention, occasional references were made to the absolutist theory of control. This attitude was referred to by Sir Robert Howard, a Whig leader, who in his speech on the state of the nation said, "I have heard 'that the King has his crown by Divine Right.'" Public discussions, however, were different in tone. . . .

At the meeting of the Convention the majority of James's followers supported the compact theory of government through which the lords and commons participated, under the leadership of the king, in the control of the nation according to constitutional precedents. Their position was revealed through the discussions of the Convention and indicated concern about the preservation of their laws, their estates, their religion, their standing in the country, and the consequences of a drastic change

in the hereditary rights of the crown. It also revealed a fear of an elective monarchy and a commonwealth. In origin it did not show a dependence upon Filmer and Harrington, but rather a relationship to the philosophy or legal principles of Richard Hooker, Hugo Grotius, the Bible, Sir Edward Coke, Sir John Fortescue, the coronation oath, and Tacitus. The speeches and writings revealed a more significant reliance upon the opinions of the learned counselors of the law than upon any other source. Those serving as counselors included Sir Robert Atkyns, Sir Edward Montague, Sir William Dolben, Sir Cresswell Levinz, Sir Edward Nevill, Sir John Holt, Sir William Whitlocke, George Bradbury, and William Petyt. In order to present clearly the political concepts of the Jacobites on the contract theory, an analysis of their opinions will be necessary.

When the Convention lords received the commons resolution, the peers requested the opinions of the counselors about the legal status of the compact theory. The majority of them asserted that, although the lawbooks did not refer to the original contract, they believed in its existence. Two of the counselors were evasive. Atkyns said he believed the term referred to the first step in government, when the king and the people formed a limited monarchy. He cited Hooker, the preamble of the act concerning Peter's Pence, Grotius, and the Bible to substantiate his opinion. When asked about the term, Dolben asserted that Coke spoke of approximately the same thing. If the principle did not exist, subjects could not demand that the king must live within the law. Whitlocke argued that the limited nature of the monarchy was derived from the king's compact with the people, and he recalled that King Alfred was limited by his coronation oath. After confessing that he had been incorrectly taught at Oxford that no contract existed, Bradbury stated that no government could subsist without an agreement between the king and the people, and he believed the body of common law was the original contract. Analyzing the body politic of England, he saw three parts: king, lords, and commons. This idea was used again and again by the lords when defending the hereditary monarchy through the concept of the original contract. Petyt emphasized the coronation oath as evidence for the existence of the original contract. After referring to the selection of rulers by acclamation in Germany, he said there was always agreement between the king and the people in Saxon times. He affirmed that, since Statute 25 Edward III, the king had been bound by his oath to rule justly. The oath, he pointed out, was administered before any subject did homage.

This uncertainty of the legal status of the original contract was reflected in the debate preceding the settlement. A pamphlet asserted, "Most men believed that the pretended Breach of that they call The Original Contract, was designed for no more than a popular Flourish." The Earl of Clarendon, however, was more profound in his analysis when he remarked at the Convention: "I may say . . . that this breaking of the original contract is a language that hath not been long used in this place; nor known in any of our law books, or public records. It is sprung up, but as taken from some late authors none of the best received." Less skeptical was the Earl of Pembroke, who outlined the character of the contract when he said: "The laws are certainly part of the *original contract;* and by the laws made, which established the oath of allegiance and supremacy, we are tied up to keep the hereditary line, being sworn to be true and faithful to the King, his heirs and successors; whereas the old oath was only to bear true allegiance to the King. There (I take it) lies the reason why we cannot (of ourselves) without breaking that contract, break the succession." A more penetrating deduction was expressed by Nottingham, who denied the ability to destroy the compact. Granting a breach of the contract, he insisted that the next in line could not inherit the crown because an individual cannot be

heir to a person who is alive. Furthermore, he pointed out, by accepting a dissolution of government and selecting a new line, the Convention would commit "the same fault we have laid upon the King." Accepting the analysis of the Oxonian Bradbury, he saw the English government as a body politic consisting of three parts, with the king as the leader of the lords and commons. With the removal of the sovereign, the remainder of the government was endangered. "For they are knit together in their common head; and if one part of the government be dissolved, I see not any reason but that all must be dissolved." A similar point of view was expressed by a pamphlet, which in discussing conditions in England emphasized the distinction between parliament and the Convention. Because the latter was not called by writs (a function of the king), it had no legislative powers.

By accepting the compact idea of government as a means for the preservation of the hereditary monarchy, the Bishop of Ely agreed with Bradbury's analysis of the body politic. The bishop conceived the compact as an agreement made when the state was first instituted. In the agreement were the conditions under which the government (king, lords, and commons assembled) should function. The body politic was obliged to make new laws and to alter old ones. Among these was a law of succession, which was as much a part of the original contract as any other statute. In the case of abdication, the disposition of the crown would not be a prerogative of parliament until all the heirs had abdicated. The bishop recognized the seven interruptions in the succession since the Conquest, but he cited the statutes of Queen Elizabeth and James I on allegiance as part of the contract, which required obedience until altered by a lawful parliament. By observing these principles, he believed England would avoid an elective crown.

In the commons, the Jacobites analyzed the nature of the government, in the case of drastic changes, with a concern equal to that of the lords. Heneage Finch believed the destruction of the contract would be a serious act. The problems created by the breakdown of the constitution would be almost insurmountable. If James were no longer king, he believed, the throne should be filled with the next in line of succession. It was true that the king could forfeit for himself, but he could not resign or dispose of the inheritance. In the case of James, his escape did not seem a complete renunciation. Yet the English people would endanger their security by sending proposals to James. Finch believed a satisfactory solution for the preservation of the contract would be to establish a regency during the life of the king. A more liberal view was taken by Sir Christopher Musgrave. Adhering to the ideal of the hereditary monarchy as an element of the compact, he believed the king could violate the contract and not destroy the constitution. To avoid disturbing the constitution, he would follow the dictum of the Bishop of Ely in distinguishing between the right to, and the exercise of the right to, the crown. The third point of view was expressed by Sir Thomas Clarges. He supported the idea of hereditary right and believed that to declare the crown void would have unusual results. It would disturb the constitution by changing the status of the king. Filling the vacancy would be more serious. Clarges thought the selection of a successor to James would convert the kingdom into a commonwealth. This development would imperil the constitutional principle of hereditary rights.

The commons as well as the peers supported the principle of a hereditary king and expressed apprehension of instable government if the lineal succession were disrupted. Although the number of Jacobites was not great in the commons, this point of view was advanced by Finch, who in a debate on January 28 expressed his belief in the hereditary nature of the crown with descent through an uninterrupted lineal succession. The king, he thought, might give up his position as in case of malfeasance of office, but in that event he would relinquish only the exercise of the crown. His departure would cause transfer of governmental control into the hands of his successor because the king could not lose his title or inheritance.

In the upper chamber the Jacobites, holding ideas much like those held by the Tories, took views similar to those held by Finch. Many of these concepts were formed upon the putting of the question "whether king James having broke that Original Contract between him and his people, and deserted the government whether the throne was thereby 'vacant'?" One group stoutly maintained that the "king never dies." The concept of a hereditary king, however, was amplified in the conference between the lords and commons in an effort to iron out their differences. Clarendon and Nottingham were the principal defenders of the lords' position. Replying to the aged Sir John Maynard, the former said, "I think, no act of ours can alter the lineal succession; for, by all laws we now have in being, our government appears to be hereditary in the right line of descent: And upon any descent, when any one ceaseth to be King, allegiance is by law due to his heir as successor." When asked by Henry Pollexfen, a house conferee, who should succeed James, he queried, "Must it not be supplied by those that should come if he were dead?" Uneasy about the status of the crown because the commons had indicated that they did not want an elective crown, Clarendon stated that a breach in the lineal succession at this time might act as a precedent which would make the throne perpetually elective. Another of the conferees, the Earl of Nottingham, discussed the nature of the crown by citing cases from English precedent. Nottingham was an ardent disciple of hereditary right. In analyzing the position of the king, he contrasted it with the status of the commoner. Because the inheritance of the commoner can be halted by an attainder, it is weaker than the royal line as defined by the lawyers of Henry VII. The status of the crown had been defined by the statute dealing with the king's succession during the reign of Henry VIII. By this law, said Nottingham, succession was limited to the king's children. If the king chose to relinquish his position, his act would not exclude his heirs. Furthermore, Nottingham, relating incidents from history, demonstrated how, in cases of disturbed succession, claimants had not taken the throne unless they had "some specious pretence of an hereditary title to it." In this manner he revealed that the throne might be vacant as to a particular person, but it would not be to the successor because the English laws recognized no interregnum. Upon the death of the ruler the next in line is the sovereign at one and the same instant. The coronation oath, in the mind of the Jacobites, did not greatly alter the hereditary position. Clarendon further amplified this condition by relating the regal position to the oath. He explained that the king must live within the law before as well as after the oath was administered. In this way allegiance is due from subjects as soon as the crown descends upon the next in line by succession. A more complex view of the oath was presented by a pamphleteer who wrote, "Though the King do not perform his Coronation-Oath, yet his Subjects are not therefore absolved from the Oath of Allegiance; and on the contrary, the King is bound by his Coronation-Oath, though his Subjects do not keep that of Allegiance." These concepts provided the foundation for the resolution for the regency in spite of the more conservative ideas expressed in other pamphlets.

The position of the Jacobites in the house of lords as well as in the commons followed with amplification the ideas expressed by the learned counsel of the law on the question of the regency. The discussion of the possibility of a regency was begun in the upper house when the commons resolution on James II was received, although doubts were expressed about the status of the king in relation to the regency. Turning to the Civil War precedent, the incident was cited wherein the commons had enacted a measure to execute the king, and the lords had rejected it on December 29, 1648. This position was sustained from the legislation, Statute 22 Edward III, which resolved that the king has no peer in the realm and cannot be judged by men. The status of the king was further clarified by the statutes of Henry VI's reign, which stated that the king could not dispose of his kingdom. Although John had tried to subvert the crown, he could not do so. In view of these doctrines, and considering the flight of James, it was concluded that the best remedy for the situation would be a regency, since it came nearest to meeting the requirements of the law. The counselors were then asked for an opinion on the legality of the regency. Sir Robert Atkyns replied that in law the regent is a guardian and a protector. If royal power were assumed, the regent would differ little from a king. With these opinions as background, the Jacobites waged the struggle on the question of the regency in both the lower and upper houses, but the idea was more widely accepted in the latter than in the former. In his debate on the state of the kingdom in the commons, Finch proposed the establishment of a regency during the lifetime of the king. An acceptance of the plan was urged because of the stability it would provide. Although Finch thought James should not be given regal powers, he was certain a sound administration would result. These ideas did not win the approval of the commons, but they were accepted by a near majority in the house of lords. A resolution for a regency during the life of James II was introduced in the upper house by Nottingham, and its introduction was followed by a long and bitter debate. Nottingham, the leader of the discussion, by citing the instance of Don Pedro, who was regent while the king of Portugal yet reigned but did not rule, exercised great influence upon the peers. His ideas did not prevail, however, as the resolution failed to carry by a narrow margin of two votes. The failure of the motion to pass made necessary the consideration of the legal position of the exiled king.

Although the commons accepted the idea that by fleeing James had abdicated, the lords, adhering to the hereditary concept of the monarchy, believed the king could not abdicate. Their position was determined in part by the analysis of the abdication principle by the counselors of law. Four of them agreed that the term was not found in common law. Atkyns pointed out that the term was included in the dictionary, while Dolben asserted that it was used in Roman law. Whitlocke and the more profound Bradbury agreed that the term could not extend beyond the person involved. Furthermore, the circumstances of James's flight were closely related to the opinion of his status. It was widely believed that, because the king was in danger, his action could not be defined as an abdication. There was, indeed, much evidence to support this analysis because a portion of the army had deserted and the remaining forces were of slight value. Furthermore, the subjects expressed a strong resentment against the king, and disorders were widespread as William's army swept inland. Under these circumstances the Jacobites believed James had withdrawn to protect himself and his family. His hasty departure had precluded the appointment of officials to administer the government. "And since his Majesty had sufficient Reasons to withdraw, these can be no Pretence for an Abdication: For we are to observe, That to abdicate an Office, always supposes the Consent of him who quits it. That this is the significration of the word Abdico, appears from Tully, Salust and Livy; to which I shall only add the Learned Grotius, De Jure Belli . . . where he makes Abdicating the Government, and plainly Giving it up, to be Terms of the same importance." Grotius, however, had been more explicit when he

added that a "Neglect or Omission in the administration of Government, is by no means to be interpreted a Renunciation of it." In addition to referring to foreign authors, cases in English history were cited. "We have but two Instances with us, which looks like an Abdication since the Conquest; which are the Reigns of Edward II and Richard II both which were unjustly Deposed by their Subjects. However they did not renounce their Allegiance, and declare the throne Void, till they had a formal Resignation under the Hands of both those unfortunate Princes."

In the commons the proponents of these opinions were Lord Charles Fanshaw and Sir Thomas Clarges. The former in a talk on the state of the nation observed that the king had been forced out of the kingdom because of fear of his own subjects. Clarges could not accept the principle of abdication. Following precedents, he believed the principle referred to voluntary action.

The opposition of the peers to the application of the abdication principle to James revealed opinion similar to that of the counselors, the pamphleteers, and the commoners. Theirs was largely expressed in the conference with the commons by Nottingham, the Bishop of Ely, Rochester, and Clarendon. Upon the receipt of the commons resolution on James II, the lords refused to accept the principle of abdication. Their reasons were given in a resolution returned to the house of commons, which stated that, as the term was unknown in common law, the lords desired to use a word upon which there was general acceptance. It was pointed out that, when the term was used in civil law, it indicated a voluntary renunciation. Obviously, James had not left voluntarily. The free conference between the lords and commons brought greater amplification on the nature of abdication. Although the three major speakers, Ely, Clarendon, and Nottingham, presented conflicting details in analyzing the principle, they agreed that the word was not found in common law;

that when the word was used in civil law, it meant voluntary action; and, if the principle were applied to James II, the hereditary succession would be endangered. Their major concern appeared to involve the declaration of a vacant throne.

The lords were apprehensive about the use of the word "vacant" to describe the condition of the throne. This concern probably developed from the reluctance of the counselors to render exact opinions. They were evasive and vague. Atkyns, Levinz, and Montague believed the question could not be answered by reference to common law but was a case for the high court of parliament. Although agreeing with the other counselors that the decision should be made by the high court, Bradbury was willing to speculate on the principle. He believed that a vacancy might exist, and, if the royal family were extinct, he thought there would be no question about it.

Using Bradbury's statement as the foundation, the peers vigorously opposed the commons resolution on the vacancy. While considering the resolution, the lords struck out the clause "and that the throne is thereby vacant." In a statement sent to the lower house, the lords explained their rejection of the word "vacancy" on the following grounds: "1. Because, by the Constitution of the Government, the Monarchy is Hereditary, and not Elective. 2. Because no Act of the King alone can bar or destroy the Right of His Heirs to the Crown; and therefore . . . if the throne be vacant of *James* the Second, Allegiance is due to such Person as the Right of Succession does belong to." Not much was added to these statements by the speakers at the free conference. The Earl of Nottingham refused to accept the idea of vacancy because of its consequences. If the condition applied to James's heirs, the crown would be elective. Clarendon went further in his thinking about the results of declaring the throne vacant. In a debate

with Pollexfen he asserted, "If then you say this government is vacant, that would be to put all those by that [i.e., to remove all those who] should take the succession." Furthermore, he believed the nation might become a commonwealth. The Earl of Rochester, commenting on the difference between hereditary and elective governments, observed that in the former, upon the death of the occupant, the "next heir was immediately in the throne." This was not the case in elective kingdoms: "Indeed, in *Poland* when the king dies there is a vacancy, because there the law knows no certain successor: So that the difference is plain, that whenever the monarchy is hereditary, upon the ceasing of him in possession, the throne is not *vacant*: where it is elective, 'tis *vacant*." The Earl of Pembroke, however, was willing to recognize an expediency to solve the problem. Explaining his position, he said, "We should make it a case of demise of our kings, as our law calls it; that is, the king is dead in law by this Abdication or Desertion of the government, and that the next heir is to take by descent."

On the question of the vacancy as well as on previous issues, Clarendon stated that it was the general belief among fair-minded men that the Jacobites had the most logical arguments. Disregarding the legal and philosophical case advanced by the supporters of James II, however, the Whigs and their Tory allies forged ahead to depose James and to elevate William and Mary to the English throne.

Throughout the interregnum the Jacobite political concepts had developed along a pattern that would preserve the continuity of the constitution. The bulk of their ideas that were advanced in the debates, public and official, were based on legal and constitutional precedents and on the opinion of the learned counselors of law rather than on the divine-right theories and practices of the early Stuart period, as has generally been assumed.

Reappraisal of John Locke's Relation to Revolution Theory

PETER LASLETT

Peter Laslett is a Fellow of Trinity College, Cambridge. In addition to his important work on John Locke, he has published an edition of Sir Robert Filmer's *Patriarcha*. Currently, he is at work on an analysis of the social structure of England in the seventeenth century.

JOHN LOCKE received the following letter from the Hague on 31 January 1689, whilst he was waiting in Rotterdam for a ship to take him home, now that his exile in Holland could come to an end after the Revolution:

I have been very ill this fortnight. The beginning was what is called the disease of one's country, impatience to be there, but it ended yesterday with violence, as all great things do but kings. Ours went out like a farthing candle, and has given us by this Convention an occasion not only of mending the Government but of melting it down and making all new, which makes me wish you were there to give them a right scheme of government, having been infected by that great man Lord Shaftesbury.

The writer was the wife of Locke's friend, Lord Mordaunt, one of those who had been in Holland helping to bring the Revolution about. Mordaunt himself was now in England with William, Stadtholder of Holland, who was already in military and political control of the country. The "Convention" she mentions, the Convention Parliament, was working out the constitutional future of England after James II had spluttered out. By 11 February Locke was in London: on the 12th the Declaration of Right was completed: on the 13th William and Mary were offered the crown.

This letter, except perhaps for its last phrase, aptly expressed the traditional view of the reasons why Locke sat down to write *Two Treatises of Government*. The book has 1690 on its title-page. The year 1689 had been one of wavering in the face of a dangerous reaction, which threatened to make of the first Revolution in the history of the modern world just another dynastic usurpation accompanied by an appeal to the turbulent Estates. What was wanted was an argument, along with a scheme of government, an argument deep in its analysis and theoretical, even philosophical, in its premises, but cogent and convincing in its expression. *Two Treatises* presents along with its constitutional scheme an argument of precisely this type. The object of its author and the occasion of his authorship are set out just as might be expected in its Preface. He wrote to "establish the Throne of our Great Restorer, Our present King William; to make good his Title, in the Consent of the People, and justifie to the World, the People of *England*, whose love of their Just and Natural Rights, with their Resolution to preserve them, saved the Nation when it was on the very brink of Slavery and Ruine."

The traditional case, then, for supposing that the composition of this work belongs wholly and indissolubly to 1688, the year of the Glorious Revolution, is superficially convincing. The book contains passages which refer unmistakably to the political events of the eighteen months between the

From Peter Laslett, "The English Revolution and Locke's 'Two Treatises of Government,'" in the *Cambridge Historical Journal*, vol. XII, No. 1, 1956. Reprinted by permission of author through Curtis Brown Ltd.

change of the seat of power and the time of its publication, and one statement which dates itself. It is a wonderfully effective justification of what the people of England had done in the year before its appearance, and of what they were going to do in the years to come, indeed of their political behaviour for the following century and more. It gave coherence to their new constitution, it crystallized their social and political beliefs, it rationalized their Revolution then as it rationalized the American and French Revolutions which came after. Statements like these are a standard feature of all the history books and the works on political theory, for Locke on the English Revolution is the supreme example of the way in which political event interplays with political thinking. This belief has never been seriously doubted there since his book appeared, and it is far too deeply engrained, far, far too useful, to be easily abandoned. Nevertheless, it is quite untrue.

Untrue, that is to say, in its most useful form. What Locke wrote did justify "the Whig Revolution of 1688," if that phrase can be permitted at all. It is quite correct to assume that some of the text was written in 1689 to apply to the political situation then. What cannot be maintained is that the original conception of the book was to justify a revolution which had already been consummated. A detailed examination of the text and of all the evidence bearing on it goes to show that it cannot have been the events of 1688 which fastened Locke's attention on the fundamental nature of society and politics, political personality and property, the sacred rights of the individual and the ethical imperatives on government. The conjunction of affairs which set his mind working on these problems must be sought at an earlier period. *Two Treatises* in fact turns out to be not the rationalization of a revolution in need of defense, but a demand for a revolution yet to be brought about.

This is the view of its historical occasion which will be presented here, and an attempt will be made to establish its connection with the years 1679–81, when a Revolution, an abortive Revolution of the peculiarly English, constitutional sort, was being contemplated. Some of the evidence will be taken from the papers of Locke, only recently made available, in the Lovelace Collection in the Bodleian Library, supplemented by the study of what remains of Locke's library, books from which the present writer has been able to examine and borrow. But much of it comes from the content of the book itself and from historical circumstances which have both alike been always open to investigation.

It must be said at once that the fallacy we have attacked is not supported by Locke's biographers. H. R. Fox Bourne published the longest and still the most authoritative *Life* as long ago as 1876 and made the following assertions on this subject:

It is probable that in 1681 or 1682 Locke prepared the first of the *Two Treatises* published in 1690, and more than he then published. Though what is now the second essay may possibly have been prepared in England in 1689, its tone and method seem to suggest that it was composed before, instead of after, King William's accession. . . . On these grounds, supported by some minor considerations which hardly need here be set forth, it may be fairly assumed that the whole work was substantially completed during the last year of Locke's residence in Holland.

It is a pity that he did not go into his minor considerations, but it seems clear that the men who have so glibly repeated the traditional account of the occasion of the book, have done so without consulting the standard biography.

This account focuses attention on two features which the superficial student has little reason to notice, because he practically never sees the book in anything like its original form. They are these: that it consists of two separate books, the first of which breaks off unfinished in the middle of a sentence, and that Locke wrote a Preface stating that over half of what he had originally composed had been lost. The first book has only once been reprinted since 1884, and that in the most unsatisfactory of all editions, though the most used. Even this edition omits Locke's Preface, which, though it is indispensable for the proper appreciation of the occasion of the work, has never appeared in any edition at all since the year 1824. When we treat what we are pleased to call our great political classics like this, there can be little wonder that a minor mythology should have grown up around one of them.

I have quoted from the Preface the words in which Locke expresses the hope that the book would serve to justify the Revolution, but he is mainly concerned there with the writings, the influence and person of Sir Robert Filmer, a figure of wonderful obscurity and doltishness, or so he deftly suggests. He tells us that the *First Treatise,* described on the title-page as a refutation of Filmer, had originally been much longer, twice as long again. Nothing he says refers directly to the time at which the work was composed, but, since he goes on to explain why it would not be worth his while to rewrite the work at its original length, we may take him to imply that the polemic against Filmer had been written some time before, and was not so much a thing of the moment when the Preface was composed. This fits the chronology. Filmer's great vogue had been seven or eight years earlier and only the lingering attachment to his principles of the passive obedience party in the Church justified the appearance between the same covers of the *First* and *Second Treatise.*

This evidence, reinforced perhaps by allusions in the text and tiny scraps in Locke's papers, evidently led Fox Bourne to the view of the date or dates of composition which we have mentioned. Recent specialist students of Locke have followed him. They have freely granted that the *First Treatise* was written before his Dutch exile began late in 1683, and they explain the fact that it contains the only statement which incontrovertibly belongs after the events of 1688 (the reference to Judge Jeffries) as an insertion of 1689. But the second book, they seem to agree, must be much later, and can belong only to the months immediately before and the months immediately after the Revolution, though, with certain exceptions, it is not easy to see which passages preceded or succeeded it. They have noticed that the very few books which Locke directly refers to were all in print before 1683. But in the absence of any complete knowledge of the editions and copies which Locke actually used for the purpose of the *Second Treatise* and in general, they have not interpreted this fact as pointing to an earlier date for the second book. They see nothing impossible in supposing that Locke wrote this second book in its entirety between February and August 1689, when it must have been complete for the Licenser's stamp on 23 August, except that the drift of his statements makes it look as if the Revolution was yet to come. Their general position seems to be that to press for too definite an occasion for the writing of the book is to detract from its perennial value as political philosophy. It would seem that if it cannot be shown to have been occasioned by the English Revolution, it must not be allowed to have an occasion at all.

After this there is very little left of the traditional view. But before it is abandoned, it should be pointed out that there is evidence in its favour which has never been brought forward. In some ways it provides a far better explanation than the one just summarized. If the wording of Locke's Preface is considered carefully, it will be seen that he refers to the work as a whole; he does not imply that it was written in two parts and on two different occasions, separated by some years. It is "a Discourse concerning Government," with a beginning, a middle (now missing) and an end, not two disparate essays, one a fragment, brought together for common publication. His cross-references within the text tend to confirm that this was his view of it. They all occur in the first book, which is an interesting point to which we shall have to return. In §66 he talks of something he will examine "in its due place," which turns out to be the second book §§52–76: in §87 he talks of acquiring Property, "which how he could do will be shown in another place," namely in the *Second Treatise*, Ch. 5: in §100 he says "for which I refer my Reader to the Second Book." The first words of the second book are "It having been shewn in the foregoing Discourse," which means the preceding part of the work in progress, not an earlier and separate "discourse," for that word is reserved for the complete work.

These points may look over-refined, but the fine details of Locke's own references to his own writing are important in view of Dr. Gerritsen's very interesting discovery, made by the exact use of the subtle methods of analytical bibliography. He has shown that the title-page to the second book was a later insertion in the course of printing, which may imply that the title-page to the whole, printed later, was brought into line with it. It follows from this that Locke may not originally have thought of his volume as in two parts at all, any more than any work divided into two "books." The word "Treatise," the expression "Two Treatises," the title "An essay of Civil Government" applied to the second book, were all afterthoughts, appearing on the title-pages, and not used in the text, even in the cross-references. What Locke thought he was writing was a whole Discourse, presented for his own literary purposes in two books.

Now the general difficulty of this discussion is its unreality. No one can tell how long a "historical occasion" lasts, and it does not make sense to question historians about it. The phrase "The English Revolution" is already commonly used to cover the years after 1688 up to 1714, and to cover many other things as well as periods of time. If we permit ourselves this sort of latitude, there is no difficulty in making the occasion of the "Revolution" which gave rise to Locke's political phi-

losophy include the years 1679–87 also. The recognition, then, that the span of time taken up in the actual composition of *Two Treatises* was relatively short makes very little difference to the general issue. But it does make possible an exact chronological argument about the work Locke put into it, the work of original creation that is to say, as distinct from addition and revision. If it can be shown that any considerable part of it can belong only to the situation of a few particular months, then the whole belongs to those months.

A straightforward demonstration that the complete book was composed between 1679 and 1681, or 1683 at latest, can be made from the obvious connection of the *First Treatise* with the controversy over the republication of the works of Sir Robert Filmer. It is well known that the ability of the Monarchy and the Monarchists, or Tories as they were beginning to be called, to withstand the attacks of the Exclusionists, or Whigs, was due to their superior journalism and propaganda. Dryden, L'Estrange and the Tory pamphleteers won a striking victory over Shaftesbury and the Green Ribbon Club. The most successful move which they made was undoubtedly the resurrection of the works of this forgotten Royalist knight, who had published absolutist, patriarchal tracts between 1648 and 1652, and who had left his *pièce de résistance*, the *Patriarcha*, in manuscript. I have tried to show elsewhere how rapidly the collected works of Filmer became the *ipsissima verba* of the established order after their republication in 1679, *Patriarcha* being added to them in 1680, when there was a second issue of the tracts.[1] Locke's *First Treatise*, as we have seen, is a sentence by sentence refutation of the whole body of Filmer's works. Moreover, the exhaustive contradiction of patriarchalism runs right through the *Second Treatise* too. This is perhaps the most important

---

[1] Laslett, 'Sir Robert Filmer,' in *William and Mary Quarterly*, 3rd series, V, no. 4 (October, 1948), and Filmer, *Patriarcha*, ed. by Laslett (1949).

result of editing it critically. If the *First Treatise* belongs to these earlier years, and if the *Second Treatise* is part and parcel of it, then the whole work was written before 1683, and there is an end of it.

Though a simple proof of this sort carries conviction to an editor of the book, there are points at which it can easily be attacked. The impression that the book was written as a whole, and is not the result of two separate impulses from historical circumstance, is a matter of critical opinion. It might be granted that the whole work was completed in some form as early as this, but maintained that it was so modified later as to be in fact a book of dual or multiple composition; moreover, Locke's practice with his other works could be used to confirm this view. It could be asserted that Filmer and Filmerism were not issues confined to the early 1680's, but were still very much alive in 1688 and 1689, and even later. If so, the argument could be that the book was composed as a whole, but at this later period, or (for an author in a hurry could certainly have done it) between February and August 1689.

These possible objections make it necessary to go further into the evidence. Some of it can certainly be used against the view taken up here. The claim that as late as 1689 it was still necessary for a Whig writer to go to some trouble to refute Filmer is, of course, correct. Filmer was still being reprinted in 1696, and any acquaintance at all with English political literature up to 1714 will show that Locke was not wasting his publisher's money by including the *First Treatise* in his book. James Tyrell, who knew Locke best as a political writer, had published his *Patriarcha Non Monarcha* against Filmer in 1681, but he found it necessary to return to the attack in 1692. Locke's book reached Oxford early in December, 1689, and when Tyrell saw it he thought of it as an attack on patriarchalism, "a very solid and rational treatise cal'd of Government in which Sr. R. Filmers Principles are very well confuted." In the previous June the English Quaker Furly who had been his host in Rotterdam and was now in England wrote thus to Locke:

I met with a scrupulous Cambridge scholar that thought nothing could discharge him of the Oath of Allegiance that he had taken to James II and his successors. I had pleasant sport with him upon Sir R. Filmers maggot.

But all this goes to show why it was that Locke published what he had written against Filmer in 1689, rather than to demonstrate that he actually wrote his refutation then. It is just possible that a man could find time to do all that Locke is known to have done between February and August of that year, and also to compose a work at such length against the patriarchal extremists. The study of the tracts he acquired makes it quite plain that he interested himself in everything that was written for and against the new regime at that critical time. But it seems extremely unlikely that he allowed himself to be rushed into print in this way, even by circumstances of such supreme importance to him, and even more unlikely that he lost over half his manuscript. Locke was not a man to mislay great bundles of papers, or to permit a printer or publisher to do such a thing. Nor was he a man to do things in a hurry. He never printed his first thoughts on any subject; certainly not on one as important as the foundations of society and the grounds of obedience. It took him nearly thirty years, from his late twenties to his late fifties, to produce in print a single one of the works which made him famous. For nearly all of them we have his drafts, notes and letters which cover the whole of this period. The book on Education was composed as a series of letters spread over the years of his exile. Although we do not possess such a series for his major work on Government, it seems impossible to believe that they did not once exist. To think of Locke as a man who could write a rationalization of events which had just taken place is to misunderstand his personality. It would have been a psychological impossibility for him to do so.

The view that the work was composed at leisure in the Lockeian manner in the later years of his Dutch exile, say in 1687–8, the last successive draft of it being ready for the printer by 1689, is no more than guesswork. It accounts for the tone of its political comment, which, as Fox Bourne said, reads as if it was made before William's accession. It allows for an even earlier date of germination. In its favour is Locke's connection with the men who made the Revolution, who, as we have seen, might have expected him to write about it. There is some correspondence of his of 1688 about printing a work which could just conceivably have been this one, but was more probably the philosophical *Essay*. Locke was being pressed from England as early as 1687 to publish his work on toleration, and this might be made into an argument by analogy for the *Treatises*, since Locke on *Toleration* did appear in England in 1689, though he disclaimed responsibility. There is even a scrap of MS. evidence which might be used to show that Locke was working at the text of the *Second Treatise* in February 1687, for he noted in his diary on the 2nd of that month an extract which is found in §14. But it is quite certain that it only found its way into the printed text in the course of publication, for it appears in the later state of the first edition and not in the earlier. This detail, then, may indicate only that the text was in existence in this area at this date, and suggests that Locke did not have it in his possession at the time, but copied his note into it two years later, in 1689 when it is known that he modified what he had written in many places.

It is to the very considerable body of evidence which we have about Locke's reading, his lists of books and his books themselves, their whereabouts and the notes he made on them, that we must turn for positive evidence to prove that *Two Treatises* was complete in some form by 1683. But before we do this we may refer to some obvious and very superficial features of the text of the work itself. In 1689 the words "King James" with no number following could mean one thing only— King James the Second. Yet in the text he had printed in that year Locke refers twice to "King James" when he meant James I, surely a very significant anachronism which he corrected in later printings. It seems strange that this has not been pointed out before, but even stranger that the parliamentary issues and events of the years of the Exclusion Controversy have not been noticed in the constitutional discussion of the *Second Treatise*.

Except, perhaps, in his last chapter, Locke's first concern there is with the summoning and dissolution of Parliament. This was for him the critical relation between Legislative and Executive. It was this which could lead to "a state of War with the People" when the "Executive Power" shall use force to hinder the *meeting* and *acting* of the Legislative." Now this was an issue in 1689, but it was between 1678 (or even 1675) and 1681 that it was really crucial. It was then that Shaftesbury, with Locke at his side, had made attempt after attempt to force Charles II either to dissolve a parliament long out of date, or to summon it after an intolerable series of prorogations. The *"long Train of Actings"* of §210, which became the "long train of abuses" of the American Declaration of Independence, includes the underhand favouring of Catholicism ("though publickly proclaimed against)." Now this "acting" was that of Charles II, not James II. James did not find it necessary either to be underhand in favouring Catholicism, or to proclaim against it. . . .

. . . As early as 1679 Locke had begun a work on Government, which was to have as one of its objects the criticism of Filmer. But the work he had begun, and which he had written at least as far as §22, was not the *First Treatise*, but the *Second Treatise*. The *First Treatise* seems to have been begun later, perhaps six months later or more, when the influence of Filmer had grown so dangerous that a full length examination became necessary to Locke, and had indeed already been undertaken by Tyrell and Sidney. The change of plan as well as the writing of the whole work can be attributed to very particular political and personal circumstances. They come from the events of the Exclusion Campaign of 1678–81, and from Locke's association with the protagonist of that political drama, the first Earl of Shaftesbury.

It is this detailed evidence, refined but exact, which suggests the view of the literary structure of *Two Treatises* here put forward. It does not require minute analysis of Locke's text to feel the force of the suggestion that the *Second Treatise* is the earlier work. As it stands, the printed book is cumbersome and forbidding, two hundred unreadable pages introducing an essay which is lively and convincing, if a little laboured and repetitive. We can see why Locke arranged his material thus, though we may feel aggrieved at his insensibility. But there is no good reason for supposing that he thought his thoughts in such an improbable order, or wrote them down like this. Every one of his positions is assumed in the *First Treatise,* but, as we have seen, when he refers to them there he has to send us forward to the *Second.* There is never an occasion to do the opposite. Who would deliberately choose to begin the exposition of a complicated theme by the refutation of another man's system without laying down his own premises? And who would choose to do it not logically, step by step, as Filmer's other critics do, but seriatim, by the pages and paragraphs of a motley assemblage of his occasional writings?

We cannot now do more than suggest this new approach to the book. The question of how complete the *Second Treatise* was when the *First* was begun must be left open. So must the complicated problem of the re-writing and re-arrangement caused by this change of plan. But I believe that the *Second,* the positive statement, was substantially written down when the *First,*

the negative commentary, was begun. I believe also that this is the only satisfactory account of the manner of composing the complete book. It can only be valid if it is granted that the whole was written up to ten years earlier than is usually supposed. John Locke's *Two Treatises of Government* is an Exclusion Tract, not a Revolution Pamphlet.

This is as much as is now certainly known and can safely be inferred about the historical occasion for the writing of *Two Treatises.* It leaves a great deal of room for conjecture. Here only one guess will be made, but if it is a lucky guess it explains a very great deal.

There is a document referred to in Locke's papers and in Shaftesbury's papers which had a history corresponding quite exactly with the history of the manuscript draft or drafts of *Two Treatises* as it has been worked out here. The great obstacle to its being accepted as identical is its title. It was called *De Morbo Gallico*—"Of the French disease" (or, the French pox), a euphemism for syphilis. Conspicuous and vulgar, it may be thought, but it must be remembered that cover names are common in these papers, especially for secret, dangerous or embarrassing documents, and, if we are right, *Two Treatises* may well have been thought of as all three. Moreover, Locke and Shaftesbury undoubtedly did think of despotism as the French disease, and when he began his work on the subject Locke had just returned from a four-year examination of the French disease as a system of politics.

When Shaftesbury's papers were seized in July 1681 Locke was in Oxford, but draft A (i) of the *Essay on Human Understanding* was not the only document connected with Locke which was listed. There was "Mr. Locke's book of fruit trees," and his letter on the Oxford Parliament. There was also "Notes out of Mors Gallicus writ in my lords hand." It has never been suggested that Shaftesbury was a syphilitic, though there can be no certainty. But whatever his lordship had noted, it seems unlikely to have been Locke's printed book with the title *Morbus Gallicus. Omnia quae extant de eo,* for it had been printed in Venice as long ago as 1566. In the census of his library at Oxford made a little later in the same month, Locke entered *Tractatus de Morbo Gallico* amongst the folios. His old medical book was a folio, but it is not likely that it would have found a place so close to his Hooker and to two folio note-books, one of them containing the original draft of his unfinished work on the Understanding. On 19 July he left for London, not from Oxford direct, but from Tyrell's house at Oakley. He often left things with Tyrell, and in his diary on the 18th he wrote—in shorthand— "Left with him De Morbo Gallico." This object then begins to look like something more important to him than a medical treatise, and a year later his medical and political friend Thomas wrote in such a way as makes it clear that it was something which Locke himself had written. "You may send your Observations de Morbo Gallico," send it to Thomas, that is, at Salisbury, and he gives the name of the messenger.

This was in July, 1682. The next reference is in the first letter he wrote from Holland after his flight there in 1683, full of cryptic allusions to his possessions left behind. It is addressed to Edward Clarke, of Somerset, his confidential friend, agent and relative.

Honest Adrian [Thomas] writes me word that the chest that is now in Mrs [Smithsby's] custody was not opened, though he had the key and directions to do it. Neither do I ask whether any thing else in her custody was opened, only give me leave to tell you that I either think or dreamt you enquired of me concerning the title of a treatise, part whereof is in Mr Smiths [?Mrs Smithsby's] hands, and it is *Tractatus de Morbo Gallico.* If there were another copy of it I should be very glad to have that at any reasonable rate, for I have heard it commended and shall apply myself close to the study of physic by the fireside this winter. But of this I shall tell you more hereafter, when I hear that there are more

copies than one, for else it will not be reasonable to desire it. I desire also to know whether Dr Sydenham hath published anything this year.

It is a treatise and it is in two halves: Locke wants another copy of one half. But no detailed sense can be made of this letter without the missing key agreed upon between Locke and Clarke. The medical references look very like a blind.

The last context is mutilated but clearer. It occurs in another but much later letter to Clarke, written in 1687:

I beg also that the half . . . [hole in original] . . . *de Morbo Gallico,* which I left with R Smith [Smithsby] sealed up in a little [?box—Rand's guess] about the length of a hand and half a hand in breadth, may be sent into . . . [gap in original].

The letter ends:

You may easily perceive why I would have that tract De Morbo Gallico.

To make it into a package of this size, Locke may have torn out the pages of the folio writing book which stood in his rooms in 1681, and tied up those he thought it safe to preserve. It is tempting to suppose that he wanted them in 1687 in view of the changing political situation.

If our guess is right, and *De Morbo Gallico* was in fact the cover name for the manuscript of *Two Treatises,* all this follows. Shaftesbury read and noted it before July, 1681. At that time it was in Locke's room at Christ Church, written in a large folio notebook, just as was his *Essay on Human Understanding.* Tyrell had it in his keeping for a little while after this, not knowing what it was. Thomas read it in 1682. By the time of Locke's hurried departure in late 1683, it had been split into two parts, and after this we hear only of one of those parts, though we have a confused hint that there may have been another copy somewhere. The fragmentary manuscript was in the keeping of the London landlady, Mrs. Smithsby, at whose house Locke lived in 1689, and who returned other things of his then. She may have kept it until that year, so that Locke never saw it between 1683 and 1689, in spite of his requests to have it sent to Holland. This fits in with the evidence that he did not modify the work before that time.

We must identify this part manuscript with the whole work we now have. The other, longer, piece had presumably been destroyed before he left for exile. It was, of course, the continuation of the *First Treatise*, written, we must remember, not in the middle, but in the later pages of his original folio notebook. His motives for destroying it between 1682 and 1683 can easily be inferred. It was in this continuation that Locke, like Sidney, must have proceeded from the principles of patriarchalism to the practice of monarchs. One of the charges on which Sidney was to lose his head was exactly this, that he had identified Filmer's patriarchal monarch with the King of England and justified forcible resistance to him. Such, it is suggested, was the "Fate which" as Locke tells us in his Preface, "otherwise disposed of the papers which should have filled up the middle, and were more than all the rest."

The history of the composition of *Two Treatises* cannot be said to be very important to the study of Locke. It merely brings that book into line with the others he wrote. It shows that his character was consistent and that he left too much written on paper to conceal the story of the work, however much he may have wished to do so.

Nor will it make much difference to the general historian. The account of the relation of Locke's political system to the English Revolution may have to be modified a little. A few "befores" instead of "afters," some word like "predisposition" where "reflection" or "rationalization" now appears, this will cover the case. Exactly the same chronological revision has had to be made in the case of the absolutists, Hobbes and Filmer. Their systems of authoritarian reaction can no longer be regarded as the result of the attack upon established authority in the English Civil War. It will be as easy to accept, or to ignore, the fact that Lockeian liberalism was worked out before and not after 1688.

But the political scientist may find in this revision further grounds for being critical of one of his accepted concepts, so useful and so inclusive as to be a general category, the concept of Revolution. The name Revolution, in the sense in which we use it, was born in England in 1688–9, and it is fascinating to watch the old word for sudden dynastic change acquiring its new meaning in the political literature of those months. Because of what happened in England then, and because of the view which contemporaries so soon took of it and which historians immediately elaborated, we talk of the English Revolution, the French Revolution, the American Revolution, the Russian Revolution. We do so because we associate sudden political change with total transformation, political and social, intellectual and even aesthetic. Locke and his political theory, with his epistemology and the rest of his thinking added to it, afford the most useful of all examples of this. But as we have said, the chronology of the English Revolution has to be made so elastic if this association is to be justified, that the phrase itself has become meaningless. Locke was no revolutionary in any case, in the conventional sense. How can we go on associating him with "The English Revolution," whatever that may mean, now that we know that he wrote in anticipation of events? Perhaps it is time we abandoned the phrase itself and the system of muddled and superficial generalization which goes with it.

William of Orange: Prime Mover of the Revolution

LUCILE PINKHAM

Lucile Pinkham, born in 1904, received her A.B. from Carleton College, went on to Columbia and Radcliffe for graduate work, and returned to Carleton in 1934 to become the chairman of the history department, which post she occupied until her death in 1960.

W ILLIAM, Prince of Orange, bore a name and a title that were a part of the glorious past of his home, the United Provinces of the Netherlands. By birth and by deeds he could well be identified with that country, where he lived the first thirty-eight years of his life and where, as Stadholder Prince, he achieved a position of note in European politics. Nevertheless, as Stadholder Prince he might have been forgotten or have become, at best, a "minor character" in the *dramatis personae* of the late seventeenth century. It is as William III, King of England, that he is remembered. Names are symbols. Often they tell us not only who individuals are, but also something of what others think of them. The people of that nation where this man once reigned have, throughout the centuries, shown a disinclination to refer to him as William III, a title which would place him firmly in the roster of their accepted monarchs, but have chosen rather to use the patronymic "Orange" or the definitely foreign-sounding designation of "the Dutchman." Why is it that the English have thus refused to take this man to themselves, have considered him an outsider, whose place in their history was almost accidental?

Can it be that he has been rejected because through his mother, Mary, the daughter of Charles I, he was one of the Stuarts, that always-alien family that thought to find in England the goal of their hopes and ambitions but never realized their dreams? Not likely, for the Stuarts were either loved or hated, and to arouse those emotions is in itself a form of acceptance, one that William never achieved. A more plausible answer to our question lies elsewhere. William III came to the throne of England through a revolution that is called "glorious." Cherished in all the nation's annals, from folklore and ballad to political essay and scholarly monograph, this revolution is the proud capstone of a national tradition. Insomuch as William's contribution is recognized, by just so much must that of the English themselves be diminished. If the revolution is to remain "glorious," William must remain forever an outsider, an alien prince whose interest in what happened on the island was as incidental to his personal goals as those goals were to England.

That was not the case. When this man was crowned king he was realizing an ambition which had influenced him since his boyhood. No sudden decision nor immediate need had led him across the North Sea and down the length of the Channel to

From Lucile Pinkham, *William III and the Respectable Revolution* (Cambridge, 1954). Reprinted by permission of Harvard University Press, pp. 2–4, 16–17, 60, 126, 146–147, 156–157, 168–170, 230–233, 234–238.

accept the "invitation" of his English friends to help them submit their troubles to "a free parliament." On the contrary, his expedition was the result of plans laid carefully over many years. The setting, both in England and on the Continent, had been judiciously arranged. Public opinion had been subtly molded in his favor. Even his chosen adherents had been selected carefully for the weight they would carry for him in his struggle to win the crown. That hangers-on and potential political opponents not of his choosing found their way into his camp before the revolution was over in no way diminishes the importance of the above fact.

His significant position in English politics had been recognized for almost twenty years. The only male heir to the throne who was a Protestant, in 1677 he had married the one person whose claims seriously rivaled his own: his cousin Mary, the Protestant daughter of the Roman Catholic Duke of York. Although he married her, in part at least, because he did not wish to see her become the wife of some man who might champion her rights in opposition to his own, by this deed William accomplished a great deal more than the mere elimination of possible future disputes. He established himself throughout Europe as well as in the British Isles as the man who would one day rule England either in his own right or as consort of the Queen. . . .

. . . Let it be understood here that William wanted the English crown for its own sake much more than for the advantages it would give him in diplomatic maneuverings on the Continent. These last play their part, but a close scrutiny of them, especially of the time element, will reveal, as we shall see later, that they were more a support for the expedition of 1688 than a cause thereof, and undue emphasis upon them has obscured the significance of William's personal ambition and its relation to the outcome of the Revolution. We must not lose sight ever of the man with whom we are dealing. We must remember constantly the fact, often overlooked, that William was the grandson of Charles I and that Stuart influence had been stronger in his early life than that of his father's family. Ambitious with the zeal of an able man who *knows* that he can do better than his fellows, he had so far been given free reign in his native country only during a few terrible months in 1672. A youth of twenty-one, untrained and inexperienced alike in warfare, statecraft, and diplomacy, he had taken charge at a time when the United Provinces seemed doomed, and, relying only on himself and the magic appeal of his name to the masses of the Dutch people, he had saved the land. For thanks he won the opposition of the States General. Yet on the three occasions when he visited England he had been cheered. There he had been the darling of the Court, the sought-after companion of great politicians. England had no States General made up of proud merchants who felt themselves superior to kings and princes. In England, William could be the king he wanted to be—or so he thought in those days of the reign of James II when so many Englishmen hastened to tell him how thoroughly they were committed to his service.

Two possible courses were open to him. He could maintain the policy he had adopted in the closing years of Charles II: to wait for the natural run of events to bring him his—and his wife's—inheritance. Like almost everyone else he did not expect the interval to be long. As James was not particularly robust there was reason for thinking he would not long survive his brother. The possibility that a rival heir might be born was slight. Even more unlikely was it that James might try to divert the succession either to Anne, if she could be persuaded to apostatize, or to one of his bastard sons. Frequent warnings that this might happen were sent to William, but he was too well aware of his father-in-law's views on indefeasible hereditary right to be particularly disturbed by them. Against this policy of passivity stood William's own impatience and the imperative necessity of taking a stand. James's life expectancy might not be good, but neither was his own, for he was already in his middle thirties and his always-frail constitution did not hold out promise for too long a future. Moreover, he was beginning to receive indications from England that people there, confident that he would oppose James's policies, were expecting him to do so immediately and openly. . . .

If a passive policy was neither tenable nor desirable, the alternative was, of course, direct action. Yet should William choose this course he had to be sure he would win, for the dangers inherent in the failure of an outright assault upon the English throne were too grave to warrant the contemplation of anything but success. In addition to making as sure of victory as was humanly possible, William had to plan a campaign, in both the military and political senses of the term, which would bring him the crown without damaging too severely those very attributes which made it so attractive to him. That is, he did not want a struggle based on purely constitutional issues. Therefore his best means of accomplishing his end in this respect lay in joining forces with the discontented Tories. But like them he would have to compromise with the Whigs, with the Dissenters, and with the malcontents. He must scheme to uphold the Church of England without antagonizing the Dissenters and to protect the prerogative without losing the support of the Whigs. He must pose as the savior of the Protestant religion while he maintained his friendly associations with Catholic Europe: Spain, the Empire, and the Papacy itself. . . .

Among most of those in the immediate circle of the Prince it was certainly assumed that the crown was the ultimate objective. As early as September 1688, Simon Pettecum, who was one of those most thoroughly acquainted with William's plans, burst out impatiently to the imperial ambassador, "Of what importance is it to the Emperor whether the King of England is named James or William?" Shortly before the expedition sailed, Huygens, William's personal secretary, and brother to the famous scientist, wrote in his diary "Rooseboom discussed what would happen in England *when his Highness should be master there.*" (Italics mine.) The very casual way in which this man, certainly in a position to know, alluded to the future, is highly suggestive. There is nothing surprising to him in the possibility that William might be master of England. The assumption is to be found even beyond the immediate circle. D'Albeville wrote from The Hague on November 23, 1688, that the English in the Prince's army "took an oath amongst themselves before their departure that they would never lay down arms till they made the Prince of Orange king, and laughed at a free parliament." If he was not stating proven fact he was at least repeating current gossip. That the idea was not entirely absent even from the minds of those who remained in England is indicated by a letter dated December 2 from Sir Robert Howard to William stating that "they only fix upon hopes of remedy by a total change of persons.". . .

But it is William's own acts which are of greatest interest. In those tense days that followed the flight of James and preceded the meeting of the Convention, he expressed himself to Halifax:

Said, hee did not come over to establish a Commonwealth.

Said hee was sure of one thing; hee would not stay in England if King James came again.

Hee said, with the strongest asseverations, that hee would go if they went about to make him regent.

The implication is clear. William would have the crown or nothing. . . .

After midsummer of 1688 William's relations with England ceased to be those of an outsider. He was now a potential usurper who stood an excellent chance of becoming a *de jure* king. The significance of his position derived from the strength of his military preparations and from his refusal to make any appreciable compromise with his own followers or any compromise whatsoever with James. He was going to invade England and not once did he offer to call off or even delay the invasion in order to give the English people and their King an opportunity to settle their dispute by themselves. Any indication that a solution might be reached without his intervention simply stiffened his determination and gave new speed to his preparations. The impending invasion, therefore, was of paramount importance. Its objective was debatable; its imminence was not. No settlement could be made until it was over. Because of that the England of this autumn became a strange dreamland in which King and people acted with the futility that comes from knowing that the most vigorous activity can be rendered nugatory by decisions as yet unmade. In this interlude, more than at any time after his coronation, William determined what was going to happen in England. The English people were not free agents. They paid the piper, but William called the tune. . . .

. . . The principal line of propaganda in England . . . became that of stress upon maintaining the true laws, liberties, and religion of the country. This would appeal to everyone but the most Jacobite Catholics and most dyed-in-the-wool Tories and many of the latter were won over by the claim that James was subverting indefeasible hereditary right by a supposititious Prince of Wales. It could also smooth over factional strife, at least for the time being, as both Whigs and Tories could place their own interpretation on "true laws and liberties and religion."

Perhaps the biggest advantage, however, in insisting that his objective was to maintain the established laws was that it enabled William to claim that resistance to him was resistance to legally constituted authority. This was done by casuistry, it is true, but it worked. It formed the basis for that part of his Declaration wherein he called upon the people of England for their support. It appeared in his directions to his fleet when he ordered his admirals to inform any members of the English navy who offered resistance that they would be treated as enemies of the *kingdom* of Great Britain, thus drawing a distinction between loyalty to the King and loyalty to the nation. He used it to form the concluding and the clinching point of his appeal to the soldiers and sailors to desert the ranks of James's army and navy and join his own:

. . . I hope God will put it into your hearts at this time to redeem yourselves, your religion, and your country from those miseries which in all human appearance can be done only by giving mee your present assistance who am laboring for your deliverance.

In addition to appealing to the sentiments as well as to the convictions of the English it constituted a measure of safety against the danger of a charge of treason to those who were engaged with William, a protection, it is true, that was more illusory than real, for the widest interpretation of the statute of treason could scarcely provide foundation for it.

William left little to chance. Weeks before the invasion could be commenced he drew up not only the Declaration but also the appeals to the soldiers and sailors to which reference has just been made. When word from England indicated that the King might succeed in coming to a peaceful settlement with his people a second declaration was prepared, urging that no one be fooled by engagements that could be broken, by promises that could be retracted, and by concessions that could be withdrawn once the danger was over. Thousands of copies of all these proclamations were printed and sent over to various parts of England where they were placed in the hands of secret agents who were ordered to distribute them as soon as they received word of the Prince's landing. The equipment of the army included a printing press which was to be used for new broadsheets if the need arose. . . .

The fact that William risked his expedition on such a slender margin is indicative not only of the extent to which he was gambling his whole life on success, but also of his calm confidence of obtaining it. The way he met the problem illustrates the manner in which he arrogated to himself the rights of the head of the government and involved in his cause people who had no idea of making him king. Supplies for his fleet were obtained by the seizure of large stocks of goods kept at Plymouth to provision the English navy. Such a step was not incompatible with the right of conquest, but William did not assert that right. He claimed to represent the true authority of the country. Bolder still was his taking over the tax machinery of Exeter and the surrounding territory whereby he turned that source of James's revenue to his own use. All money in the possession of the receiver of customs was seized and officials who protested were dismissed. William Harbord, a former Exclusionist and perennial malcontent who had joined the expedition shortly before it left the Netherlands, was made paymaster of the forces, and an order was given that all revenues were to be paid to him. Three other Englishmen were set to supervise the collection of the excise. Should William be defeated these men, together with Harbord, would be hard put to it to explain their actions to their lawful sovereign. It became their interest, therefore, to see to it that William did not lose. Even before the army set out on its march toward London, Bentinck was discussing the possibility of another source of money: that all those who signed the Exeter Association should make contributions in proportion to their wealth. Such a device, if it was proposed, must have met with some opposition or objection, for it was never put into practice. Not until two weeks later was an alternative adopted. This was a voluntary loan, backed by some of the men who had by that time come to join William, notably Sir William Portman, one of the most influential leaders in the Southwest. The sums thus gathered served the double purpose of filling the treasury and of giving their donors addi-

tional motive for desiring that the venture they were financing should be successful. With these resources William made his way toward London. . . .

. . . Anyone studying the Revolution of 1688 cannot but be impressed with the way in which previously made plans for insurrection and desertion went into operation throughout the country, but he must reserve his true amazement for the way in which everything that happened, whether in his own immediate vicinity or in distant Yorkshire or Derbyshire was, ultimately, in the control of the Prince of Orange, who used what he wanted to use, discarded what he wanted to discard, and ignored, when it suited his purpose, even such old friends as the Earl of Danby himself. . . .

The insistence of the Prince on a minimum of well-defined points, first: no repeal of the Tests, and second: the decision of a free parliament, had a tremendous value, for it concentrated attention on immediate problems and left the nature of their ultimate solution in abeyance. The Whig, the Tory, and the man with no party affiliation could all join a leader with those objectives. At some point, however, there had to be a transfer of authority from the King to his opponent. This had to be done whether or not the intention was to dethrone James. It had been evident since the middle of October that no reforms or promises of reforms were going to satisfy William. He was determined that everything that was done should come as the direct result of his actions, in his presence, and as far as possible, under his direction. He claimed to represent the legally established sovereign power of England which in theory could be interpreted as capable of demanding the obedience not only of the people of the country but even of its king. Whatever James II did, therefore, could be treated with contempt unless it was done under the aegis of the Prince. Yet it was hard for most men to separate king and nation in their minds, in spite of, or perhaps because of, the Civil Wars and the Interregnum. King and people must act together. Neither was complete without the other. Only the most fanatic Whigs and those who were touched by the lingering ideas of republicanism felt otherwise. When William claimed to represent the country he was also claiming that the King must act with him. He was not deposing the King unless or until the latter refused to recognize the intangible fusion. He was merely refusing to admit that James had any authority, and opening a way whereby men, even those of rather strong Tory principles, could render obedience to himself without violating their consciences.

William had begun to take steps toward the assumption of authority before he left the United Provinces, although he did not put any of his plans into active operation before the expedition set out. First of all, there was the Declaration with its demand for a "free parliament" elected on his terms. Added to this was the postscript or "additional declaration" with its reiteration of references to a free parliament and admonition to the people of England to place no faith in the reforms that James had granted. William's orders to Herbert to treat any English seamen who tried to stop the Dutch fleet as enemies of Great Britain should also be placed in this category, although it was never necessary to put them into effect. Another action of major importance was the making of a great and a small seal bearing the English arms which were given to William's secretary, Constantijn Huygens, to use for the validation of all documents concerning English affairs. Huygens received these seals a few days before the first, unsuccessful, departure of the fleet, and retained custody of them until after the New Year when he was forced to yield them to the English William Jephson.

Immediately upon his landing William began to use the authority he was claiming to possess. Although his actions could be construed as those of a successful leader either of a belligerent foreign power or of a group in rebellion against legitimate government, it should be noted that he never for one moment referred to them as such, but persisted throughout in his assertion that he represented the lawful sovereign power in the nation. Upon that assumption he took actions that were normally reserved to the king. One of these was his order, conveyed through Burnet, to the clergy of the Cathedral of Exeter to omit prayers for the Prince of Wales. This, of course, was tantamount to ordering them to proclaim that they did not recognize the child's rights as heir to the throne. The clergy objected, but were forced to yield. The seizure of the tax machinery followed. One of the king's officers who demurred was placed under arrest. Commissions for new regiments were given out, not for a foreign army or for a rebel force, but as lawful acts validated by Huygens with the English seal. Orders were given that anyone who attempted to stop the raising of regiments by arresting men who were on their way to join the Prince should themselves be arrested and brought before Sir Robert Atkins who was commissioned by William as a justice of the peace. . . .

With . . . much irrefutable evidence that William was fast losing whatever popularity he may have had among the English at the time of his arrival, the question very naturally arises how he could have been made king even as a co-ruler with his wife. A statement attributed to Halifax, who is said to have told William on his arrival in London that "he might be what he pleased himself . . . for as nobody knew what to do with him, so nobody knew what to do without him" sums up the situation about as well as anything. James was gone. William was present. Something had to be done, for the country could not continue in a state of uncertainty. We see here also what can happen when a disorganized majority, united only on the common ground of disapproval of what is taking place, is faced by a well-organized minority which, however much it may be concealing dissension within itself, is united in its determination to reach an immediate objective. This minority had been able to gain control of the mechanism whereby that objective could be gained—the Convention. Observers and members of that Convention might note their uneasiness and apprehensive dislike of decisions being made, pamphleteers might criticize, or clergymen denounce, but none of them was in a position to do anything constructive, or even obstructive. Another factor of importance was the presence in the country of a group which wanted to overthrow the monarchy entirely, the existence of which brought about a somewhat paradoxical situation which eventually worked toward William's benefit. The republicans had assisted in the Revolution hoping that the outcome might be victory for their point of view. Once it was over, so far as the actual fighting was concerned, they very naturally turned against William. Never a serious menace, they were still of enough significance to provide a telling argument for the Orangists to convince their opponents that if William was rejected, or if, angered by continual controversy he carried out his threat to return to the Netherlands, a republic might be created to fill the political vacuum. Finally the importance of the time element cannot be too often repeated and emphasized. Not only was settlement imperative. The opposition, caught unprepared, did not have the time to organize, to sort out its own differences, and to reach an agreement upon any other solution than that which the Orangists offered.

Because the latter group controlled the Commons and were the most powerful single element among the Lords, the real debates in both Houses were upon procedure rather than upon objective, and were based on obscure legal points rather than upon fundamentals. The question of "abdicate" vs. "desert" involved the issue of whether or not James had acted voluntarily, for in principle abdication had to be voluntary. It was the fact that if "deserted this kingdom" were the chosen phrase a temporary aspect was given that finally turned the scale, for if James returned, or even tried to do so, he could no longer be said to have deserted. The word "vacancy" suggested a breach in the succession, a denial of the doctrine of indefeasible hereditary right. The issue involved here was much more serious than the other because it gave rise to the suggestion that the office of king was being made elective. When this point was forcibly advanced by the Lords we find 151 members of the Commons voting to drop the phrase. Most interesting is the fact that the doctrine of indefeasible hereditary right was far from being denied at this Convention in spite of later interpretations put upon its actions. Almost no one would admit even that what they were doing might create a precedent, and those who were willing to do so insisted that anything of an elective nature was for this time only. The contention was made that unless the throne was vacant with respect to James it could not be filled by anyone else; to the argument that it would be filled by his heir the old maxim of English law that a living man had no heir was advanced. The real significance of the question lay in whether Mary alone, or William and Mary, should be raised to the throne. On the principle of immediate succession of the heir Mary would have had to be proclaimed and it was only by going through the fiction of a vacant throne that William could be considered unless the members of the Convention had been willing to pass over both daughters of James to adopt a modified Salic law of inheritance. In making their decision, however, the Convention was acting not so much as an elective or legislative body as in their old historic judicial capacity as a "High Court of Parliament." Their job was not to make an heir, since only God could do that, but to find out who was the heir. . . .

As for William himself, he played a more direct part, once the Convention was assembled, than he had been doing for the past two or three weeks. His aims underwent a certain amount of modification for it soon became obvious that he could not have his way in his desire to rule alone when even such staunch supporters as Her-

bert were aghast at the idea. It was probably Dijkveld who influenced him here, by
pointing out that insistence on the sole
right to the crown would make him un-
popular not only in England but also in the
United Provinces and with Spain and the
Emperor. William, however, was adamant
in his refusal to consider Mary as sole ruler
or to accept any kind of arrangement
whereby his official position was contingent
upon hers. That was not selfishness on his
part, but merely common sense. No matter
how sure he might be that she would survive him, he could not afford to run the
risk involved. He knew that as Prince Consort he would be expected to undertake
and carry out foreign policies and he could
not take the chance of being left in mid-air
on any of them by his wife's death. His
diplomatic position would be intolerable.
This, of course, involved coming to some
agreement with Anne. The final arrangement—that he should have the crown
jointly with Mary during his lifetime, but
that any children of his by any other wife
than Mary should be superceded by Anne
and her heirs, seems to have been worked
out in private some days before the public
vote in the Convention. . . .

There remains only one further point:
the Declaration of Rights, the conditional
nature of which has been greatly over-
stressed. The origin and substance of this
document are worthy on their own merits
of an intensive study which cannot be ac-
corded to them here. The demand for the
declaration reflects the deep need of seventeenth-century England for clarification of
many points of its laws. This was the logical time for such a clarification to be made.
The Commons' resolution to draw up the
declaration came the day after the one on
which the resolution declaring the throne
vacant was made. A committee appointed
to draw up a first draft reported back to the
whole House a few days later. During this
period, at least up to February 7, the main
issue confronting both Houses was the
other resolution. Discussion on the two subjects, the declaration and the problem of

the succession, went on concurrently in the
Lower House, but the discussions were
curiously unrelated to each other. Certainly at no time was the offer of the crown
made directly or explicitly contingent upon
acceptance of the declaration by William
and Mary, and it is hard to find much indication of any implicit or indirect condition.
In fact, the Declaration of Rights did not
receive its final form nor was it adopted by
Parliament and given the validity of royal
approval until much later in the year, after
William and Mary had been safely
crowned for some months. A purely accidental circumstance seems to have given
rise to the theory of the conditional nature
of the declaration. Although the resolution
to offer the crown to William and Mary
had passed both houses by February 7, not
until six days later was the offer formally
made to them. In that interval certain differences in the tentative draft of the declaration were ironed out so that, by February 13, the document had been drawn up
into what was to be substantially its final
form. As far as can be discovered, however,
the delay in making the formal offer was
caused not by any problems concerned
with the Declaration of Rights but simply
by Mary's absence. She reached Westminster on Tuesday, February 12. The next
day she and her husband accepted the
crown.

William was, it is true, somewhat upset
at first by the suggestion of a declaration
and is reputed to have said that he would
not accept a crown with any strings attached to it. Here again Dijkveld is reported to have worked for moderation. Yet
a certain amount of moderating was done
by the other side as well. All new points
were carefully excluded so that the Declaration of Rights which William and Mary
ultimately approved contained no limitations not already in existence. Nor was
William accepting any theoretical principle that Parliament had an unlimited right
of limitation. He agreed to rule according
to the laws of England as every king had
done who had ever worn the crown.

There remains the task of stating some evaluation of the significance of William's connection with the Revolution. That significance lies in the fact that the original combination of William with the Tories resulted in the end in what was actually nothing more than a palace revolution. William wanted the crown; the Tories the control of the chief offices of the realm. Next to the control of these offices the principal concern of the Tories was the Anglican Church, and the meager concessions of the Toleration Act attest to the hollowness of their glib promises to the Dissenters. To this combination of the Tories with William the Whigs brought some concern for the rights of Parliament, but they too were more interested in the Staff of the Treasury or in the Great Seal than in popular rights. . . .

The only limitations which the Revolution, as embodied in the legislation of the next few years, placed upon the King were to deprive him of the already highly questionable right to suspend the operation of laws, and to make it necessary for him, through financial and other strictures, to call Parliament every year. But, because Parliament must meet and because it could control the purse, what happened was that the royal powers which the king had hitherto been able to use in the interests of whatever group he pleased, sometimes even —God save the mark—the common people, those powers now passed into the control of the landed aristocracy which could control Parliament. In that sense the long struggle that began at Runnymede turned once more in favor of the heirs of the baronial class and for a century and a half the country was more completely in their grip than ever before: the historic counterweight to them, the royal power, was ineffective. The view that the Revolution was essentially aristocratic has been attacked on the ground that the common people supported it. That this assertion cannot be accepted without rather strong qualifications has already been indicated in those parts of this study which deal not only with William's unpopularity but also with devices that were used in such places as York to trick an otherwise loyal populace into taking part in an uprising. Yet even if the assertion could stand unqualified, judgment should be based on results, not immediate participation. Of course many of the "mobile" as they are called in the letters and diaries of the leaders, were enthusiastic. Even if they had not been overmastered by anti-Catholic hysteria they still would have welcomed the prospect of improvement in their daily lives. But the benefits of the Revolution did not go to them. . . .

The Revolution Justified by Divine Right

GERALD M. STRAKA

Gerald M. Straka, born in 1931, received his undergraduate degree at Wisconsin State College, Milwaukee, continued work at the University of Virginia, the University of Wisconsin, and the London School of Economics. He is the author of *The Anglican Reaction to the Revolution of 1688* (1962). Currently he is Assistant Professor of History at Michigan State University Oakland, Rochester.

SINCE the days of Macaulay and the great reform bill, a number of historians have been at work revising the Whig interpretation of the Glorious Revolution. Just as Magna Carta was placed in its proper mediaeval setting, clearing it from the misty precedential motives of seventeenth century parliamentarians, so the Revolution Settlement has been placed more and more in its Stuart setting, freeing it from nineteenth century positivism. Unlike the case of the former, however, the revolution era has not as yet been treated in a single volume incorporating all recent revisions of thought. David Ogg's book comes as close as most, but nearly every new survey, when it mentions the revolution, still repeats the old liberal view, as if the work of the past thirty years had never been accomplished.

Among the vacuous banalities that one finds in revolution rhetoric is the statement that divine right theory died a sudden death in 1689. Of course, those who declare this have in mind—or should have in mind—the divine right of hereditary succession; and, although they might seem to be right, it can be argued that the House of Orange, being in the succession, could claim the divine right of heredity. What is usually meant by the death of divine right, however, is the death of divinely constituted monarchy, and for this there is little evidence. Certainly some minor figures like Charles Blount and John Wildman, as well as a number of court sceptics, derided monarchical divinity, but these were few compared to the majority of Englishmen who did not believe that when James II fled the throne he took God with him. The writings of Bishops Lloyd, Stillingfleet, Tenison, Burnet, scores of pamphlets and books by Anglican laymen indicate that divine right continued to exert an influence on men's minds greater than that of a nostalgia for a dead idea. No doubt contractarianism and natural rights gained an ever-growing ascendancy in political thought after 1688, but this is no reason for ignoring the fascinating development within the divine rightist school. The contractarians have too long given a one-sided view of revolutionary doctrine and we must be made aware that the ardent Anglican who believed in Charles's and James's right could do no less than allow William his divine right to rule. It is my belief that divine right in a new form went just as far as natural right in giving support to the revolution and that it stood midway be-

From Gerald Straka, "The Final Phase of Divine Right Theory in England," to be published in a forthcoming issue of *The English Historical Review*.

tween the non-religious views of Locke and the super-religiosity of the nonjurors.[1]

Jonathan Swift once remarked that every Englishman above the age of forty believed in the sacredness of Queen Anne's person and in her divine right to rule. But in what sort of divinity was it that the post-revolution Anglican believed? If he read any of the numerous volumes on the subject of divine right or if he, like the pious John Evelyn, attended the parish church at least three times weekly during William and Mary's reign, attended to the sermon or read the sermons in print, he probably believed in some version of what I choose to call the divine right of providence. It is this divine right of providence that replaced the Stuart concept of divine hereditary right and characterized the political theory of the post-revolution Anglican and his church.

From the summer of 1688 and through the winter of early 1689, the church found itself less and less able to cope with a revolution that it had to a large degree started. Sancroft, the archbishop, had presented a number of "matters . . . judged necessary for his Majesty's Knowledge and Consideration" to James in October, and because it smacked of an ultimatum, James had rejected it. If he had accepted the church's terms, William might have been spared the cost of his expedition, for they were not unlike a first draft of the bill of rights, asking among other things for a "fair and free Parliament . . . to sit to redress all Grievances, to settle matters in Church and State upon just and solid Foundations, and to establish a due Liberty of Conscience." But James fled to France in the face of William's army, and Sancroft, to the consternation of future historians, refused to have the same terms put in force by the new government. Sancroft had played

much the same part with James as Langton had played with John, but unlike his thirteenth-century counterpart Sancroft had the divine right homilies of the Jacobean church on his conscience and these clearly forbade rebellion against the Lord's anointed. What Sancroft would not carry through, men like Tillotson, Tenison, Burnet, Lloyd of St. Asaph—all episcopal creations of the revolution—accomplished, and while Sancroft became the leader of the quixotic nonjuring church, the main body of Anglicanism maintained a church, alike in all respects to what Sancroft deeply desired except in its political theory.

Were Anglican leaders under William therefore a pack of trimmers? Did they in fact repudiate divine right in order to save their livings in the national church? Macaulay said they did and Trevelyan hinted as much. So did the nonjurors. Was it so? Let us look at the situation through the eyes of the Revolution Anglican: a national church threatened with disestablishment for want of its leaders' ability to take the oath to the new sovereign, a body of dissenters waiting to fill the offices of all those deprived of their livings because of the oath, the very foundation of the principles of Cranmer, Hooker, and Andrews— good and true principles about the nature of primitive Christianity and the unity under obedience that it enjoyed with the Roman state as the national religion—all in jeopardy. And above all there was the fear that the new church, if disestablished, would abandon the belief of the prophets of old that God was concerned directly for the political management of His earthly vassals. Divine right was far more than a dogma: it was the inarticulate conviction of the peasant and yeoman, the Squire Westerns and Mr. Allworthys who had been raised in Elizabethan piety to believe in the partnership of God, King, and Country.

The new appeals to laws of nature found among the contractarians, associated as they were either with Hobbism or the writings of the regicides of 1649, were

[1] The nonjurors were those who refused to take the new oath of allegiance to William and Mary. Most of them were in the Anglican Church. They maintained that James II was still king and refused to admit that parliament had a right to change the hereditary succession. Some nonjurors became Jacobites when they actively sought James's restoration. [Editor's note]

anathema to the average Anglican. The church of the Restoration, believing the king was God's vicegerent on earth, preached with unlimited vigor that it was mortal sin to rebel against him. It thus became the job of the revolution church to show how none of these beliefs had been violated by William's accession, that all Anglicans could assent to the new government without losing their souls, and that it was indeed imperative for them to follow divine right, passive obedience, and non-resistance to the throne of William and Mary. James II was to be recognized for what he was, while on the throne, a divine right king of England. But inasmuch as he had misused his holy trust by personally accepting the headship of the antichrist of Rome, by politically accepting the leadership of the tyrant Louis XIV of France, and by subverting the religion and liberties of England, God had judged him unfit, had raised up a new David as a providential deliverer, William of Orange, to avenge Him and save His church. So William, the church declared, held his crown *de facto* after the manner of Henry VII, enjoying his title as conqueror in the trial by battle and as God's chosen instrument of punishment and salvation.

The theme of providential delivery, full of biblical and historical precedent and imagery, became the favorite theme of revolution church oratory, casuistry, and biblical exegesis, and during William's reign assumed as much importance in church writings as the subject of non-resistance enjoyed after the overthrow of Cromwell's commonwealth in 1660. . . .

. . . National observances in the church calendar perpetuated the habit of thinking in terms of historical providences: "Witness an Invincible Armado [sic], threatening our Kingdom with perpetual Slavery of Soul and Body, dispers'd and ruin'd by the irresistible Power of God. . . . Witness the dark designs of Hell [the Gunpowder Plot of 1605], to destroy our Laws and Law-makers, our Church and State at one blow, betrayed and confounded by a

kind of supernatural, and prophetical impression. . . . [These proved] there is not any Church on Earth, that has had more Signal Providences, to approve it the immediate Care and Concern of Heaven, than that we are Members of." Gunpowder Day and 29 May, the restoration of Charles II, especially were annual repetitions of the old providential theme. It was even demonstrated how Henry VIII fitted into the grand scheme, for this "high-spirited Prince, a zealous Assertor of the Popish cause, and a Writer against Luther," laid the foundation for a rapid reformation since his personal quarrel with the pope was used by providence to establish the Reformed Church of England.

As the Anglican observed providence at work in history and the perfect balance it seemed to maintain between evil and good, a doctrine emerged that providential miracles always reflected the essential goodness and perfection of God. The consequences of any historical act were the measures of providence's intention, for providence was not mere fortune or caprice. Good would be rewarded and evil punished by some agent—natural, human, or divine. The divine justice was most commonly expressed by the word "judgment," a singular act of punishment by God for a sin that might or might not be known by the sinner. Wars, famines, plagues, any of these could be judgments. Robert Fleming's *A Discourse on Earthquakes, as Supernatural and Premonitory Signs to a Nation* (1693), was a curious mixture of fact and religious interpretation rendered as judgments. The year 1692 had seen an earthquake in London, frightening some into thinking that there would shortly be "heavy judgments from Heaven." Through pulpit oratory people had become familiar with the judgment that was Cromwell's reign, the plague, the great fire, the Dutch war, and the more recent judgment, the reign of James II. Yet however severe the judgment, decisions "were always designed for wholesom and excellent Ends," for providence did not mean the mere permission of God. Even in the grossest evil could be found the "most glorious designs of God's Grace and Providence . . . even the Crucifixion of our Saviour himself" or the bloodless victory of William over James.

The churchmen of the revolution, then, considered providence as a hierarchy of divine causes: on the lowest plane it ruled nature and the universe; it considered man and his general history; finally Christianity, Protestantism, and the Church of England. Since the church was under the temporal guidance of the state, then providence's ultimate concern was believed to be tied to affairs of government: "If God demonstrate his Providence in anything here in this World, . . . he exercises it in the Governing, Defending, and Protecting of public Persons and Societies." Atterbury echoed such thoughts when he said, "since the Age of Miracles ceas'd, as it did, when the Testimony of the Gospel was fully Seal'd, the chief way, in which God hath been pleas'd to give Extraordinary Indications of his Power and Providence, hath been by such Signs of the times, such Wonders of Government" as the age's great political upheavals. Such great changes were God's way of achieving "Political Justice." Of course, there was ample biblical justification for these views since Jehovah's direct intervention in the governments of Saul, David, and Solomon provided the church with its fundamental justification for providential political theory. Biblical history, combined with a scholarly knowledge of the providential history of European courts, led churchmen to the conclusion that since the actions of governments affected the well-being of all souls, God's primary point of concentration was on politics, where the battle of good and evil assumed epic proportions. In great public transactions "God has reserved to himself a transcendant Right (as it were a Court of Equity) . . . to mitigate that rigorous procedure, and redress those unequal Judgments [of human politics], which might otherwise reflect upon his Wisdom or his

Justice." God's governance of the world was thus taken in its most literal sense, and the theoretical foundation was laid for the assumption that William III had as much divinity in his kingship as the man whom he had dethroned.

The translation of providence from the theological to the political scene was undertaken by every Anglican cleric from Canterbury's Tillotson to St. Paul's new Dean, William Sherlock, who, after a year of soul-searching, took the oath to William and Mary and robbed the nonjurors of one of their ablest theoreticians. Sherlock's *The Case of the Allegiance Due to Soveraign Powers* (1691), now generally forgotten, was the first major work in the new field of providential divine right and was its most controversial exposition. Sherlock was not completely original in his formulation, for the providential conquest and deliverance was a theme that had been in the air throughout the autumn and winter of 1688–89. He had been hard at work on the idea, however, during the summer of 1690, and by August the major lines of its development were clear to him. He based his entire argument on biblical writ and on the great Jacobean compilation, Bishop Overall's *Convocation Book* of 1606. In brief, his argument ran:

God governs the . . . world, removeth Kings, and setteth up Kings, only by his Providence; that is, then God sets up a King, when by his Providence he advances him to the Throne, and puts the Sovereign Authority into his hands; then he removeth a King, when by his Providence he thrusts him from his Throne, and takes the Government out of his hands: for Providence is God's Government of the world by an invisible influence and power, whereby he directs, determines, over-rules all Events to the accomplishment of his own Will and Counsels. . . .

There were many ways by which a dynasty could be established: by hereditary claim, by election of a people, and by conquest, which Sherlock thought was the most common form of establishment. In matters of succession there were two main categories:

"Divine Entail" as in the biblical sense of a direct grant from God, and "Human Entail" made under constitutional procedure; ". . . but all these ways, or any other, that can be thought of, are governed and determined by the Divine Providence, and the Prince thus advanced is . . . truly placed in the Throne by God. . . ." Thus Sherlock added a new dimension to divine right by maintaining that there was no theological conflict between a legal entail derived by hereditary right and possession derived by conquest: "It is all but Providence still, and I desire to know why the Providence of an Entail is more Sacred and Obligatory than any other Act of Providence, which gives a Setled [sic] possession of the Throne?" The central idea that Sherlock kept in mind was that all power is from God (Romans 13), and if this divine pronouncement which had been the basis of Stuart divine right were true in the case of one sovereign, it was true in others. Babylon and Egypt had ruled over the chosen people by God's judgment just as Saul, David, and Solomon had ruled over them by His mercy. The distinction between kings *de jure* and *de facto* related only to the laws of the land, but in the light of providence all kings had God's authority if their reigns were sanctioned by God. Regardless of the human legal right of one king over another, the great court of heaven had overruling jurisdiction in its providential acts against which man was powerless. God's primal concern with government for the sake of human society meant that His judgment could not err, neither could it be resisted.

A companion work to *The Case of the Allegiance* was Bishop William Lloyd's *God's Ways of Disposing of Kingdoms* (1691). Not only was this work more consistent with the traditional view of divine right, but it exhibited an erudition beyond anything Sherlock could muster. Lloyd took for his text the verses from Psalm 75, "For Promotion cometh neither from the East, nor from the West, nor from the South. But God is the Judge; He putteth down one, and setteth up another." What gave his book thorough respectability was that the glosses were complete with elaborations from no less an authority than James I, remarkably suited to the English revolution: " 'Though no Christian ought to allow any Rebellion of People against their Prince, yet doth God never leave Kings unpunisht when they transgress these Limits.' " Lloyd also linked providence more closely with the responsibility of kings to God: "As a Judge, [God] administreth Judgment and Justice both which are said to be the habitation of his Throne. Particularly when he decrees a Conquest of any King or Kingdom; it is either as a Judgment on them for Offences against himself, or it is by way of Justice to others whom they have injured." Just as the temporal power of the sword to enforce justice cannot be denied, "so of God, that when he puts down one, and sets up another, he doth it as a Judge, even [as a] judge among Gods."

The providential theory of the geographer and government licenser, Edmund Bohun, less sophisticated than that of his preceptors of the cloth, was yet the most common Anglican approach to providential theory. Bohun believed quite simply that the providence of God watched over pious princes to preserve them from violence, while those who degraded their office by becoming tyrants were not allowed to end their days in peace. "We are safe," he affirmed, "if we do our Duty, and submit to and pray for those Powers that we find set over us, by Men as the Instruments, by God as the great Disposer of Crowns. . . ." And this was by far the most popular expression of the divine right of providence, appealing to the people's desire to lead quiet, safe lives in timeless resignation to the ways of kings and courts. The right and wrong of an issue mattered little compared to its reality; "sometimes [God] builds us up, and sometimes he pulls us down; but whatever is the success, God is the Author, and Kings are but the Instruments of the Revolution: Which as it is too mysterious for us to understand, so 'tis too sacred for us to oppose."

This application of divine right of providence theory had obviously arisen from the necessities imposed upon the church by the revolution. When Lloyd or Burnet talked about the irresistibility of providence's disposal of kingdoms, they obviously meant that a providentially ordered revolution must not be opposed. Although their ideas did much to pacify a potentially hostile Anglican element, shrewd critics were not wanting. The nonjurors tended to reject providential divine right; the dissenting contractarians tended to ignore it. It may have been perfectly true that the Old Testament proved regal authority to be founded by divine providence, but some said this method of sacred investiture had such a peculiar relation to the biblical government of Israel that it could not be applied to any modern constitution unless it could be proved beyond doubt that a divine designation had been made. It was vital, then, to prove providential right in the revolution. Theory and fact had to be linked. The first step taken in completing the linkage was in the definition of what constituted a providential cause:

First, When it is so surprizing a work, that we can assign no other Cause, from which it does, or can proceed, but God only. Secondly, When, beside the unaccountableness of the Cause, we see the effect is such as we may reasonably believe that God is concern'd for. Thirdly, When we see there was a great and near danger of losing that which God was concern'd for, if this had not happened for its preservation. I think these three that I have named are sure tokens by which we may Judge, without danger of mistake, that any thing that happens in this manner is of God's doing. [From a sermon by Bishop William Lloyd]

That there had been danger to the Church of England during James's reign, none could dispute. Everyone knew what had been feared—that the destruction of the church and the subversion of English liberties would bring ruin to Protestantism

and liberty all over Europe. The popish plan seemed so clever, carried forward with such subtlety, that when the church finally became aware of the danger, it seemed that Catholicism must surely triumph. Then suddenly the plotters broke through the bonds of secrecy and propriety, attempting to carry off liberty and religion at one stroke. "We may remember we were given up for lost by all our Friends in Europe, and did think so to ourselves it being then impossible for us to imagine from whence our Relief should come." And yet, Burnet asked, "Why went [the Jesuits] so fast and so barefac'd? Why grasp'd they so much all at once? Why was the Hook so ill covered when the Bait was thrown out? . . . In a word, all this blasting of Counsels, and defeating of their designs by their own means, was of God, and must be owned to be his doing." This was the first proof of God's ordering of the revolution: the exposure of the Jesuit plot by its own impatient zeal.

The events of the revolution supplied the real arguments for a providential right. On 23 December, scarcely a week after the Prince of Orange had entered London, Burnet set the tone of future providential sermons by preaching before William on the text, "It is the Lord's doing, and it is marvellous in our eyes." Flushed with victory, Burnet told his auditors, "We have before us a Work, that seems to ourselves a Dream, and that will appear to Posterity a Fiction: a Work about which Providence has watched in so peculiar a manner, that a Mind must be far gone into Atheism, that can resist so full a Conviction as this offers us in favour of that Truth." He declared that God had deliberately prospered the Catholic powers in order to unite Protestant Europe against them; God had united the usually divided Dutch to a complete support of William's undertaking. Then he asked the worshippers to "consider the steps of Providence . . . the Prodigies and Miracles of Providence, that have attended our Deliverance. . . ." Burnet was not speaking to an unsympathetic audience, for the providential theme had been common from the time when William's plan of invasion was first rumored; even in the autumn of '88 some men regarded it as a deliverance sent from heaven. In the week William entered London many of the clergy offered prayers of thanksgiving that "God in his wonderfull mercy has freed us from Slavery both in body and soule by this great and noble Instrument." Many people marveled at the "protestant wind" that not only blew William's sails westward but kept the English fleet in port. Burnet and many others took the wind as a certified sign of divine intervention. Tillotson studied the case of Job, who had submitted to the divine providence, and the question God had posed to him, " 'Hath thou entered into the treasures of the Snow? hath thou seen the treasures of the Haile which I have reserv'd against the time of trouble, against the Day of Battel and War.' " Thus the archbishop was led to the conclusion that one way in which providence worked was through control of the weather, as in the case of William's kindly wind. Bishop Patrick of Ely, struck by the same phenomenon, felt that God "turned the Winds . . . to be so favourable; that if they had been absolutely at [William's] own Disposal, he could not have commanded them to be more obsequious to him, than he found them. For when he was brought to our Coast by a strong Gale, in a very speedy Course; and had over-shot his Port; the Wind changed immediately, and brought him back to his desired Haven." Lloyd, however, made the most of providence by stating that no matter what William's personal motives in seeking the English crown, God had singled him out to be the instrument of James's judgment; though William might not have intended it, Lloyd was sure that God had chosen William to be England's saviour. The bishop gave even greater credit to the winds, saying, "They directed him which way to sail. They chose him a landing place, the best perhaps that could have been found in this Kingdom." As if

to bear out these assertions, from the little town of Ruan-Minor in Cornwall, came the story of how, on William's coronation day, although the town's church was locked up, the bells rang "for severall hours in great harmony," and when it was observed that no one pulled the bell cords, it was felt that "the noise was rather in the aire than in the Steeple." Another sign of heaven's favor? The month, day, and year of William's landing at Torbay were also auspicious. The day before had been their majesties' wedding anniversary, as well as William's birthday: "Shall I call this our Birth-day? or rather the day of our Resurrection?" Tillotson's impression was

That God seems in this last deliverance, in some sort to have united and brought together all the great deliverances which he hath been pleased to work for this nation against all the remarkable attempts of popery, from the beginning of the Reformation. Our wonderful deliverance from the Spanish invasion designed against us, happened in the year 1588. And now, just a hundred years after, God was pleased to bring about this last great and most happy deliverance. That horrid gun-powder conspiracy, without precedent, and without parallel, was designed to have been executed upon the Fifth day of November; the same day upon which his Highness the Prince of Orange landed the forces here in England, which he brought hither for our rescue. . . .

Finally, the swiftness of William's success seemed so sudden and surprising, that nothing but an almighty hand could have performed it, "none but [God] who fram'd the Machine, and understood the several Movements of it, could so unexpectedly, and with so little noise, have shifted so important a Scene in the World's great Theatre; . . . [it] is a thing that cannot be parallel'd in History, and which can only be resolv'd into the over-ruling Providence of God."

With the exception of the few days in London when the usual business of the city was disturbed by popular demonstration against the Catholics after James's flight, there was no period of lawless anarchy or even of sporadic fighting against William's advance guard. So peaceable was his succession, so universal was the acceptance of his actions, that churchmen looked upon the nation's sudden convergence on the issue of the revolution as a miraculous union of minds. Some obstructions there were, but the wonder was there were not more. Had this comparative unity been providentially achieved? It was known that providence frequently worked through the hearts of men, redirecting human purposes to a concurrence with the divine will. The insufficiency of human planning was an ancient theme, especially in political affairs, "because it depends upon so many contingent causes, any one of which failing the best laid design breaks and falls in pieces. . . . Besides an unaccountable mixture of that which the Heathen call'd Fortune, but we Christians [call] by its true name, the Providence of God . . . does frequently . . . confound the wisdom of the wise, and . . . turn their counsels into foolishness." More than this, God frequently controlled men's thoughts to achieve His purposes. He was commonly supposed to have done so at the restoration, and what God could achieve once, He could do again, for

It is Opinion that governs the unthinking sort of Men, which are far the greatest part of the Body of a Nation. And when all these go together, they are like the Atoms of Air, which though taken apart they are too light to be felt, yet being gather'd into a Wind, they are too strong to be withstood. But he that brings the Winds out of his Treasures, he also governs these, and turns them which way he pleases. It is the same great God, that rules the roaring Waves of the Sea, and the Multitude of the People.

For Burnet, it was "a presage of Moderation in our whole proceedings, that even the less governable Part of the Nation, I mean the unruly Multitude, has been so happily restrained from extravagant acts of fury: for without justifying what they have done, we may well rejoyce for what they

have not done, and that Bloody and Outragious Sacrifices have not been made." There was thus good reason to suspect that providence had been at work in bending men's wills to a support of the revolution.

The lords and commons were not insensible to the value of providential theory, either as divine truth or as propaganda. Upon the framing of the Bill of Rights, a clause was inserted which met with no opposition: "the said lords spiritual and temporal and commons, seriously [consider] how it hath pleased Almighty God, in His marvellous providence and merciful goodness to this nation, to provide and preserve their said majesties' royal persons most happily to reign over us upon the throne of their ancestors. . . ." When the proclamation was read, it was affirmed, "Whereas it has pleas'd Almighty God, in his great mercy to this kingdom, to vouchsafe us a miraculous deliverance from popery and arbitrary power; . . . our preservation is due, next under God, to the resolution and conduct of his highness the prince of Orange, whom God hath chosen to be the glorious instrument of such an inestimable happiness to us and our posterity. . . ."

A revolution that had been providentially directed had to be providentially protected. If there was any danger that the forces of evil would triumph in a counter-invasion, it certainly would be to God's benefit to protect the fruits of His political creation. With William leading the Protestant cause against the French powers of darkness, the war against James II and Louis XIV took on the nature of a crusade. With each success, first in Ireland, then on the continent, the view became general that the crusade was blessed. The victories of the Boyne and at the siege of Limerick first caught the church's attention. William's personal command of the Irish campaign, his many escapes from death, and his victory over the renowned arms of France, indicated to Lloyd that heaven had been with the king. Could anyone imagine how things must have gone had there been no William to assist the salvation of England? At Mary's death, Jurieu, the great French Huguenot leader, published an eloquent *Pastoral Letter* in England in praise of the providential success of the revolution. When William's life was nearly taken at Turnham Green, the author of *An Impartial History of the Plots and Conspiracies Against the Life of His Sacred Majesty, King William III* showed how "God bared his Arm, [and] shielded his Anointed and our Deliverer" time and again. Bishops Patrick and Moore compared the exposure of the 1696 plot to the providential discovery of the Gunpowder Plot, and other churchmen exhorted the nonjurors to "no longer work to combat the workings of Omnipotence. . . . 'Ye shall not go up to Fight against your Brethren, for this Thing is from [God]. . . .' " The treaty of Ryswick in 1697 gave the final seal of approval to the revolution, for not only was James II's claim destroyed by Louis XIV's forced recognition of William, but the collapse of mighty France itself was regarded as a providential wonder.

The argument for a providential revolution had its dangers, of course, and Anglicans were warned not to look on the mere seeming favor of providence alone as a sufficient argument of the goodness of any cause. The divine right of providence was a means of continuing in a modified form the more personal divine right of kings, and Robert Jenkin, Master of St. John's College, Cambridge, did a masterful study of Sherlock's providential possession theory with this point in mind. His criticism, although on the whole favorable, was honest enough to admit that the new divine right was actually an able effort to keep a rightful king, James II, from the throne by a subtle modification of the theory that had made him once powerful in his kingship. Divine providence, furthermore, was an argument fit only for revolutions and other extraordinary occurrences. In normal times, Jenkin pointed out, a steady diet of providential theory would be too unsettling for the running of any government which

must continue its business under ordinary laws. Yet providence was an attractive argument which even the nonjurors could use when they talked about the fact that Queen Mary had become mortally ill in the very month that "her Father labour'd under an unnatural Rebellion," and that she died in "the Month wherein she was proclaimed." But this was a feeble use of a theological argument that the church employed to better advantage. It must be remembered that providence was not the whole of the Anglican revolution theory, but a necessary supplement to its legal position. The doctrine of right by conquest and the *de facto* monarchy was the legal side of Anglican justification, designed to show William's right under law; the justification by providence was purely a theological position aimed at balancing the legality of William's conquest with a greater moral right. The constitutional precedents established by Henry VII's reign, if used as its sole argument, would have left the church liable to a charge of machiavellism; but with William's right to the throne granted morally by God's greater designs, no Anglican need have refrained from supporting the new government. This point perhaps explains why the idea of providence enjoyed a brief but intensive period of consideration during the years of William's reign. If a casuist like Burnet admitted "how dangerous and deceitful an Argument this from Providence will ever seem to be," he also would be sure that the groundwork was well laid in theory as well as fact before a providential revolution could be proved. The church was equal to the task, for providence was still the age's leading concept of natural and historical causation into which the revolution easily fitted:

. . . there is such a Chain in all things, the most Important matters taking oft their rise of turn from very inconsiderable Circumstances, that it is certain that either there is no Providence at all, or that it has no limits, and takes all things within its care. Yet God having put the whole Frame of Nature under certain Rules and Laws, the greater part of Providence is only the Supporting and Directing of those Beings that do still act according to their own Natures; and in these, tho' Providence is less discernable, yet it is still the Spring of the whole Machine, which, tho' covered and unseen, gives motion to all the parts of it. There are other more solemn Occasions, in which some second causes are raised above their own pitch, and are animated beyond the ordinary rate. . . . This has never appeared with more eminent Characters than in the Revolutions of States and Empires, in which both the course of Natural Agents, the Winds and Seasons, and the tempers of men's minds, seem to have been managed by such a direction, that not only every thing, but every circumstance has co-operated to carry on Great Designs in such a Conjunction, that those who observe them with due attention, are forced on many occasions to cry out 'This is the finger of God! This is the Lord's doing!' And we may the more certainly conclude, that such a Systeme of things is the effect of a special and directing Providence, when the tendency of it is to advance some Design in which the Honour of God is more particularly concerned.

Could any Protestant deny that the revolution, in destroying papal tyranny and restoring the Reformed Protestant Church of England, had not been to the honor of God?

It is extremely difficult for us to see much merit in what appears to our scientific eyes to be so much theological froth. Nevertheless, the writings of Sherlock, Burnet, Lloyd, and others were responsible, as in the case of the Jacobitical Sir John Bramston, for bringing over large numbers of thoughtful Anglicans to a full support of the revolution. On the other hand, powerful Jacobite efforts to restore James II were neutralized by the church which continued to remind Anglicans of their duty to maintain the peace, obey the law, and resist the temptation of rebellion against William's government. It was enough, as with John Evelyn, for those who at heart decried the callous disposal by parliament of their sacred crown, to be obedient Christians if they could not be patriots. The divine right of providence was an Anglican theory aimed primarily at achieving Anglican loyalty for William and Mary by demonstrating that God had given a greater right to rule than the mere hereditary. Thus the Stuart concept of divine right through blood succession was broadened when Sherlock declared that hereditary rights were no holier than providential entails.

The Anglican justification shows that divine right did not cease to be a political force after the Revolution, as so many aver, but marks, if the last, a most vital stage in the history of divine right thought in England. Divine providential right had its roots deep in mediaeval and Renaissance political theory and should be interpreted as a justification of the revolution such as an Elizabethan or Jacobean mentality might formulate. It appealed to an older but still potent piety. Seventeen years after the revolution providential right appeared in the curious work by Fleming, *The Divine Right of the Revolution*; thirty years after 1688 when the historian Laurence Echard looked back in his *History of the Revolution*, he confessed, "I always thought the Revolution to be a great Deliverance; and I have the more readily asserted it in this History, because it was not only the Opinion and Declaration of the Lords and Commons, Lawyers, and chief Divines of the Nation, but also of several who had the Misfortune not to comply with the Establishment that immediately succeeded it." In the course of the eighteenth century providential right as a justification for the revolution was to fall before the law of nature in politics as enunciated by Locke. But for this very reason Locke's justification, totally ignored by every Anglican polemicist under William, was to mean far more to the generations of the age of reason than it did to those who had lived through the Great Rebellion and the Glorious Revolution. The generations which had been raised on the Anglican homilies of the Caroline church and works like *The Whole Duty of*

Man believed that divine right was part of the rarefied structure of kingship. The question of a king's title to them and to their church was ever above the purview of the subject; the approval of providence working either through normal succession or through conquest was the only means by which a king, be he Henry VII, James I, or William III, could be granted his divine right to an English crown.

SUGGESTIONS FOR ADDITIONAL READING

Of course the student of the Revolution era should begin by reading in their complete form the works from which selections have been drawn for this collection: Ogg's *England in the Reigns of James II and William III* (Oxford, 1955); G. M. Trevelyan's *The English Revolution, 1688–1689* (London, 1956); Lucile Pinkham's *William III and the Respectable Revolution* (Cambridge, 1954); and Straka's *Anglican Reaction to the Revolution of 1688* (State Historical Society of Wisconsin, Madison, 1962). Macaulay's *History of England from the Accession of James II* is in an Everyman's Library edition. The article by Peter Laslett can be found fully developed in the introduction to his edition of Locke's *Two Treatises of Government*, the last word on the subject.

The following works place the Revolution in the broader context of the seventeenth century: John B. Wolf's *Emergence of the Great Powers, 1685–1715*, part of the "Rise of Modern Europe" series, discusses general European developments of the time. Leopold von Ranke's *History of England Principally in the Seventeenth Century*, vol. V (Oxford, 1875), is still the best constitutional survey written in the nineteenth century. J. R. Tanner's *English Constitutional Conflicts of the Seventeenth Century* (Cambridge, 1928) is a useful brief coverage. Richard Lodge's *History of England from the Restoration to the Death of William III* (London, 1910) provides substantial coverage of political chronology. It is part of the "Political History of England" series (vol. VIII). The first volume of W. E. H. Lecky's excellent *History of England in the Eighteenth Century* (London, 1892) should be consulted for his views on the Revolution. Harold J. Laski's *Political Thought in England from Locke to Bentham* (London, 1955) covers political theory. Sir William Holdsworth's *History of English Law*, vol. VI (London, 1924), provides the fullest constitutional coverage of the age. Sir Charles Firth's *Commentary on Macaulay's History of England* (London, 1938) provides not only a number of needed correctives, but is a fine history of the period in itself. Keith Feiling wrote an excellent history of the era when he concentrated on *A History of the Tory Party, 1640–1714* (Oxford, 1924). Sir George Clark's *The Later Stuarts, 1660–1714* (Oxford, 1949), part of the "Oxford History of England" series, is excellent overall coverage. Gilbert Burnet's *History of His Own Time* (London, 1850) expresses personal bias, but it is both a prime contemporary source and history of the period.

Special studies of the Revolution include Dudley Bahlman's *Moral Revolution of 1688* (New Haven, 1957), a stimulating account of reform activities that grew out of the Revolution. Church history is well covered by George Every's *The High Church Party, 1688–1718* (London, 1956); L. M. Hawkins' *Allegiance in Church and State* (London, 1928) is the most valuable work on the nonjurors; Charles Mullet has an interesting article on "Religion, Politics, and Oaths in the Glorious Revolution," published in the *Review of Politics* (X, No. 4, October 1948); but John Stoughton's *The Church of the Revolution* (vol. V of the "History of Religion in England" series, London, 1901) is the most comprehensive church history of the period.

Special political studies can be found in Robert Walcott's "English Party Politics (1688–1714)," in *Essays in Modern English History in Honor of Wilbur Cortez Abbott* (Cambridge, 1941); J. H. Plumb's oft-cited article, "The Elections to the Convention Parliament of 1689," in *The Cambridge Historical Journal* (vol. V, No. 3, 1937); and I. Deane Jones's *The Eng-*

lish *Revolution, 1688–1689* (London, 1931), which is a companion piece to Trevelyan's work.

Two works on the Jacobite movement should be referred to: George Hilton Jones's *The Main Stream of Jacobitism* (Cambridge, 1954); and the classic work by Sir Charles Petrie, *The Jacobite Movement, the First Phase, 1688–1716* (London, 1938).

Biographical studies on the period should include: T. E. S. Clarke and H. C. Foxcroft's *Life of Gilbert Burnet* (Cambridge, 1907), and Sir Charles Firth's "Burnet as an Historian," in his *Essays Historical and Literary* (Oxford, 1938); A. Tindal Hart's recent *William Lloyd, 1627–1717, Bishop, Politician, Author and Prophet* (London, 1952) adds a number of new dimensions to the period. John Locke receives excellent treatment in a biography by Maurice Cranston (New York, 1957). John Gough's *John Locke's Political Philosophy* (Oxford, 1950), together with Laslett's work, gives a rounded picture of the political theorist. There are a number of excellent biographies of Marlborough, Halifax, and other leading figures of the Revolution. William of Orange, the central figure of the Revolution, has an excellent biography in David Ogg's *William III* (London, 1956).

Finally, for those with access to larger libraries, much can be learned by reading selections from the great pamphlet collections of the eighteenth century: *Somers Tracts* (London, 1748–1752); *A Collection of State Tracts Published during the Reign of King William III* (London, 1705–1707); and the great *Harleian Miscellany* (London, 1808–1811).